IMAGES
of England

SALT & SALTAIRE

Dr Gary Firth

PORTRAIT AND AUTOGRAPH OF SIR TITUS SALT.

Portrait and autograph of Sir Titus Salt, *c.*1876.

For Julie Woodward, curator of the Saltaire Resource Base,
Shipley College, Saltaire

One

Titus Salt:
the Man and his Family

Originally from Staffordshire, Daniel Salt's family were traditionally iron founders but in 1802 Daniel married Grace Smithies of Morley and immediately acquired her father's dry-salting business at the Old Manor House, Morley. It was here that Grace Salt gave birth to Titus, the first of her nine children, on 20 September 1803.

Titus Salt was reared in a staunchly non-conformist household, following a life of hard work and great simplicity. He received his elementary schooling at a dame school in Morley, later attending as a day boy at Batley Grammar School. By the age of nine, he and his parents had moved into a hundred-acre farm at Crofton near Wakefield, where his father struggled to make a profit during the years of depression following the Napoleonic wars. At the age of seventeen, Titus was apprenticed to a Mr Jackson, a wool stapler of Wakefield. His father Daniel could see the potential of the expanding woollen trade in West Yorkshire at that time and, consequently, in 1822 moved his family to Bradford.

Daniel Salt's homes at Morley and Crofton had both been licensed for independent public worship. He and his family were well known members of West Yorkshire's Congregationalist community and, no doubt, they were quickly and warmly welcomed into Bradford non-conformist circles. Titus, like his father, became a prominent member at Bradford, firstly of the Horton Lane Congregational Chapel and later the Salem Chapel.

At the age of nineteen, Titus arrived in Bradford and was immediately bound apprentice for a second time, this time to William Rouse & Sons in a mill alongside the Bradford Canal. There he learned every aspect of woollen manufacture from his mentor, John Hammond. Meanwhile, Daniel Salt had set up in business as a wool stapler from his warehouse premises in Piccadilly, Bradford, and, after a two-year apprenticeship, Titus joined his father in the firm in 1824. For the next decade, the business of Daniel Salt & Son prospered. They were not afraid to innovate and introduce new materials, such as the wool of the Donskoi sheep from south-east Russia. Unable to convince Bradford spinning masters of the potential of this tough, tangled East European wool, Titus Salt was convinced he could spin the wool himself, so he leased Thompson's Mill in Silsbridge Lane and set up in business as a textile spinner. Successful spinning of this difficult wool provided Bradford with a new staple.

Salt, as chief wool buyer for his father's business, attended wool sales across England. At the sheep shearings in Lincolnshire he came across the family of George Whitlam, a wealthy sheep farmer of that county. In 1830 he married George's youngest daughter, Caroline, in Grimsby Parish Church.

Following his father's retirement in 1834, Titus Salt set up in business on his own account at Hollings Mill in the Goitside. By 1836, two sons – William Henry (1831) and George

(1833) – were born at the family home in North Parade, an extension of Manor Row. By the age of forty, Salt had made a substantial fortune, largely by means of pioneering the use of innovative fibres in the weaving of worsted cloth. With five mills in operation, he became one of Bradford's leading manufacturers and one of its biggest employers.

Much of Salt's wealth and growing reputation were made upon his 'nose' for new types of worsted cloth. The prevailing taste was for all-wool worsted cloth, which produced a heavy material with little potential for variety in design or colour. By the 1830's, fashion (i.e. ladies' dress material) increasingly swung towards 'light, elegant and cheaper articles of dress which, lacking the wearing qualities of former stuffs, were yet more showy and attractive...' Salt and his fellow manufacturers responded by the introduction (in 1837) of the cotton warp. The replacement of cotton for combed wool in the weaving process enabled Salt and his fellow nonconformist, textile rival Robert Milligan, to take advantage of the cheap price of cotton yarn at that time and to produce a high quality worsted fabric at a price affordable to the masses.

The introduction of the light mixed cotton and wool fabrics in 1837 marked a new era in the history of the Bradford worsted trade. It confirmed the town's prosperity and supremacy until the early 1870s when cotton prices escalated (due to the American Civil War), and fickle fashion once more swung back to all wool lustre goods. Titus Salt was one of several young Bradford entrepreneurs to alter the course of Bradford's staple trade, and subsequently transform the face of the town. (Others included Henry Ripley, Isaac Holden and Samuel Cunliffe Lister.) In 1836, Salt's personal contribution to this metamorphosis was his pioneering introduction to Bradford's weaving trade of the first successful use of alpaca, a long-fibred Peruvian sheep's wool, renowned for its lustrous and silk-like qualities. This involved him in adapting recently mechanised spinning machines, as well as experimenting in new dyes and convincing merchants of the cloth's saleability. Although not the first, Salt was also an early pioneer of the use of mohair from the Angora goat of Turkey, at around the same time as the introduction of alpaca and the cotton warp. By 1840 he employed agents in Peru and

Grace Salt, mother of Titus Salt.

Salt's second family home. In 1836, Titus, Caroline and their two sons moved to this house at the junction of Thornton Road and Little Horton Lane. Here were born Amelia (1836), Edward (1837), Herbert (1840), Fanny (1841), and Titus (1843). The house was within walking distance of Union Street Mills, which he had bought, and which became the nerve centre of his commercial and alpaca business empire.

Bradford, *c*.1875. The town, viewed from the north near the stone quarries of Spinkwell around 1875. Like many of his contemporaries, Salt removed his family from the polluted and smoke-ridden town centre to the green pastures of Lightcliffe ten miles away.

Crow Nest, Lightcliffe. Salt lived here between 1844 and 1858 as a tenant and from 1867 as proprietor, until his death in 1876. This was always regarded by members of the family as their family home. The old mansion had been redesigned in 1770 by the famous York architect, John Carr. On the south side of the house were several conservatories, the largest of which housed bananas, aubergines and other semi-tropical fruits, all personally grown by Titus Salt.

Titus Salt, Mayor of Bradford. Following the incorporation of Bradford in 1847, the council had to consist of one mayor, fourteen aldermen and forty-two councillors for the eight wards. Titus was one of seven aldermen who were also members of the Horton Lane Congregational Chapel (giving the aldermanic bench a distinct Radical Liberal bias). Salt was nominated a borough magistrate and was to succeed Milligan as Bradford's second mayor in 1848-1849, an eventful year, featuring working class unrest and an outbreak of cholera (killing 420 citizens of Bradford).

Methley Hall, *c*.1860. Traditionally the home of the Earls of Mexborough, and located between the rivers Aire and Calder, close to Castleford. John Savile, the 1st Earl, had converted the ancient Elizabethan house in 1766. It was the 3rd Earl (1830) who transformed it into the Gothic Revival structure which Salt leased in something of a hurry in 1858. It was in need of some repair and refurbishment, and he spared no expense, building glasshouses for his hobby of growing exotic fruit. He and his family lived here until 1867.

Titus Salt junior. Titus was the seventh child of Caroline and Titus Salt, born in August 1843. In 1866, he married Catherine Crossley, daughter of John Crossley and niece of Sir Francis Crossley, MP, of the Halifax textile firm. Like his father, he was a quiet reserved man but an able public speaker, who resumed the active duties of local political life (Liberal) once his father had retired as MP in 1861. Titus junior loved to give magic lantern shows of his frequent visits abroad. He raised orchids in the glass houses at Milner Field and he was a skilled wood and metal turner. He showed a keen interest in mechanical engineering, experimenting with the new telephone system between the mill and his home. He died, prematurely, in 1887, aged forty-four.

Catherine Salt (née Crossley). She and her husband dominated the life of the village of Saltaire, following the death of Sir Titus in 1876. She gave birth to four children, Gordon, Harold, Lawrence and Isobel. It was a measure of her family's wealth and social status that she was able to play hostess to members of the royal family at Milner Field in 1882 and 1887. On the former occasion, Edward the Prince of Wales and Princess Alexandra stayed overnight at the Salt's home, on the occasion of the opening of the Bradford Technical College. Until her husband's death in 1887, Catherine Salt was renowned for her lavish entertainment, making their home a centre of Bradford society.

Milner Field, south front. The family home of Mr and Mrs Titus Salt junior, from 1873 to 1887. Built to a design of Thomas Harris of Gray's Inn, London, the foreboding and towering neo-Gothic structure belies its internal luxury, harmony and beauty. This view of the southern facade of the house shows the orangery on the extreme left, leading to the conservatory. To the right of the central tower at ground level was the library, and to the left, with semi-circular turret, was the drawing room.

Crow Nest, *c.*1880. Salt had leased this property at Lightcliffe (ten miles from Bradford) as his family home from 1844 to 1858. There were twenty-three rooms on the ground floor alone, sufficiently accommodating for his growing family. Whitlam, Mary, Helen and Ada were all born here. The owner of the house decided to live there himself in 1858, and the Salt family were sad to leave but delighted when their father was able to purchase it outright in 1867. It came with an estate of eighty-eight acres and cost Salt £28,000. He spent vast amounts of money on its internal decoration and added several large glass houses.

Salt's coat of arms. Acquired by him prior to his baronetcy in 1869, his coat of arms is displayed here over the entrance of the Workers' Dining Room (1858) in Victoria Road. A chevron indented between two mullets, and a demi-ostrich displayed, holding in the beak a horse-shoe. The motto *Quid non Juvante* translates 'What cannot man do – God helping.'

A pillar of salt, 1888. Funded by public subscription, this statue of Sir Titus Salt originally took pride of place in Bradford's Town Hall Square (as here) until traffic congestion enforced its removal to Lister Park in 1896, where it remains today. It was unveiled by the Duke of Devonshire in August 1874, and sculpted by John Adams Acton. It shows Salt seated, holding a scroll of the plans of Saltaire in his left hand. The 40ft high canopy above was designed by the architects of Saltaire, Lockwood and Mawson. When Salt found out about the statue he joked, 'so they wish to make me into a pillar of salt'.

Titus Salt's favourite seaside resort, Scarborough, was one of several Yorkshire fishing ports raised to the status of a holiday resort in the nineteenth century. However, Scarborough since the 1600s had been pre-eminent as a spa town where a select clientele visited to take the waters and breathe the sea air. Salt made his final visit in October, only a few weeks before his death in December 1876.

According to this original funeral card, the funeral following Salt's death on 29 December 1876 took place one week later, on 5 January 1877. The family members reluctantly agreed to a public event of great ceremony. Following days of winter sleet and snow, it turned out to be bright and sunny, although slushy underfoot. The hearse and family members left Crow Nest at 9.30 a.m., escorted by a detachment of mounted police. The official procession had assembled in Town Hall Square, and the two groups merged there at 11 o'clock for the slow journey to Saltaire, via Manningham Lane, as the West Yorkshire Volunteers band played the Dead March in 'Saul'.

In Memoriam.

—:o:—

TITUS SALT,

BARONET.

Born September 20th, 1803.

Died December 29th, 1876.

—:o:—

INTERRED IN THE MAUSOLEUM, SALTAIRE,

JANUARY 5TH, 1877

The Salt mausoleum. Representatives from all the groups, clubs and societies with which Salt had been associated followed the cortege, as it passed before 100,000 spectators on its journey to the family mausoleum here at Saltaire.

Grand old man. Salt's passing was reported in every newspaper of any importance at that time, including some foreign journals. His lifetime (1803-1876) coincided with the years of economic growth in the Bradford worsted trade. With the exception of Titus junior, his sons had little aptitude for or interest in the textile empire he had created. The industrial dynasty which he coveted, survived him by only a few years and, in 1892, Sir Titus Salt & Sons Ltd (1881) went into liquidation and receivership.

Two

The Origins of Saltaire

Professor Asa Briggs, in his book *Victorian Cities* (1963), described the transformation of West Yorkshire textile towns, such as Leeds and Bradford, as they succumbed to the twin forces of large scale industrialisation and urbanisation, during the first half of the nineteenth century. He noted: 'There were few Saltaires in the Victorian age, but there could have been no Saltaire had there not been first a Bradford.'

In fact, after 1850, there were several industrial model communities like Saltaire across West Yorkshire. Saltaire was but part of a tradition of Yorkshire textile employers providing round their factories and mills, an infrastructure of social living, which included not only quality housing, but churches, chapels, schools, and a whole range of institutions suitable for working class self-improvement. These included brass bands, works outings, cricket teams, adult education, libraries and horticultural societies.

Traditionally, these paternalistic industrial communities had originated in the eighteenth-century cotton industry of Lancashire but, by 1850, several West Yorkshire mill masters had taken the idea a step further. This was in response to the urban chaos and class conflict brought on by a period of intense mechanisation in the 1820s and 1830s. For example, shortly before Salt's ideas for Saltaire, Edward Akroyd, a Halifax manufacturer, built the village of Copley, and later (1855) the model village of Akroydon, around his mills at Haley Hill, close to the centre of Halifax, as did the Crossley brothers at West Hill Park in the same town.

Professor Briggs was somewhat closer to the mark when he attributed the origins of Saltaire to the precedent of environmental decline and industrial conflict occurring in Bradford during the 1830s and 1840s. Men like Titus Salt and Edward Akroyd, despite their differing political backgrounds, were both committed to the idea of laying down a new moral order and developing harmony between the classes, following the social and political upheavals brought about by Bradford's political, moral and social problems of the 1840s. The model village of Saltaire was, as Jack Reynolds so adroitly perceived, 'to bring together old and new, to unite the paternalism of an earlier age to the technology and economic structure of a new industrial society'. Saltaire owes its existence to Salt's own first-hand experience of working and living in Bradford between 1822 and 1850.

The expansion of the worsted trade had precipitated Bradford's population from 16,000 in 1811 to 103,000 in 1851, transforming it from little more than a village to the worsted textile capital of the world. This number of newcomers stretched Bradford's limited communal resources and its undeveloped local government framework to breaking point. Unregulated mill construction had shrouded the town centre in a heavy pall of smoke, which shut out the light and polluted the air. Many of the new mill workers crowded into ancient cottages and yards, close to the factories and mills. In Bradford, these had been erected close to the town's only watercourse, the beck, which became so heavily polluted, it served as the town's main sewer. Colloquially known as the 'River Stink', its contents became so charged with sewage and excrement, that it could be ignited by the accidental dropping of a match. To aggravate this filth and squalor, there was a chronic shortage of water, most of it being sold from street corner carts at one penny for three gallons. Atmospheric pollution of this magnitude meant that working-class life in Bradford was nasty, brutish and mercifully short. Between 1839 and 1841, the average age of all those who died in the town was eighteen years. The death rate rose from twenty-six per thousand of the population to thirty-one per thousand in only five years, and the majority of these deaths were children under the age of five.

The squalid, stinking hovels, which proliferated around the growing number of mills and factories, served as homes for Bradford's redundant hand weavers and combers. Bradford's wool-combers (traditionally the elite craftsmen of the worsted industry but after 1845, badly served by mechanisation and low wages) established a Woolcombers' Protective Association, which organised and published a report of their own appalling living conditions. This described how several families might share a single cellar dwelling for the purpose of working the combed wool, sleeping and general living. Population density soared in the 1840s and was particularly high along the Goitside, Millbank and Wapping. Case 31 of the Woolcombers' Report highlights 'a family of fifteen in two rooms; beds five, females six; fifteen feet by fifteen feet; four persons at work and eight asleep in the upper room'. Frederick Engels, co-founder of modern communism, confirmed this situation when he visited Bradford in 1844,

> Bradford, which is only seven miles from Leeds, also lies on a little pitch-black stinking river and ... is covered with a grey cloud of smoke. The interior is as dirty and uncomfortable as Leeds ... Heaps of dirt and refuse disfigure the lanes, alleys and courts. The houses are dilapidated and dirty and are not fit for human habitation. In the immediate vicinity of the river, I found a number of houses in which the ground floor is half buried in the hillside. In general, the workers' houses ... are packed between high factory buildings and are among the worst built and filthiest in the whole city'.

These terrible social conditions no doubt prompted Titus Salt to take his workforce out of the town, but not before attempting to remedy the situation by creating a new town council by means of incorporation. Salt played a leading part in this political battle for Bradford's incorporation, which was eventually won in 1847. However, there was too much self-interest on the part of Salt's fellow mill owners on the council for them to approve costly improvement schemes of drainage and smoke control. In exasperation, Salt's solution was to develop independently a separate community, well out of Bradford and unhindered by fellow manufacturers.

His hand was forced into this unilateral action during the summer of 1849, when a cholera epidemic claimed the lives of 420 Bradfordians, mostly from Bradford Moor and the town centre slums. Simultaneous with the social improvement of the town, there came a deliberate effort on the part of its leading citizens like Salt to improve the moral and religious tone of Bradford.

During the nineteenth century the new, successful middle classes embraced church and chapel at a time when the urban working classes began to shun institutional religion and church attendance. Particularly in towns, this coincided with a marked increase of working-class violence, prostitution, drunkenness and anti-social behaviour. As early as 1825, an early correspondent to Bradford's first newspaper could write:

> Even the most sober walk through the streets of Bradford after dusk is such a perilous undertaking ... Bradford, of which I have now for some years been an inhabitant, is proverbially one of the dirtiest and worst regulated towns in the West Riding'.

Titus Salt was very concerned with this moral decline of his home town and, during his year as mayor, supported a public enquiry into the Moral Condition of Bradford, particularly its excessive number of brothels and beer shops. Since the 1830 Beer Act anyone was entitled to open a public beershop. For those men and women of the lower classes living in poverty and squalor, drink was often the quickest way out of Bradford, and Salt's report showed that there were more than 150 beer shops in the Bradford borough alone. Many of these had singing and dancing saloons alongside where:

> Facilities for dishonourable intercourse between the sexes are afforded and almost all are, and some are in fact, brothels under another name. It is painful to add that some public houses and hotels scarcely take a higher moral position than beer houses.

Undoubtedly, Salt was disturbed by the details of this report, and concerned to provide a well-disciplined environment where middle class values of respectability, thrift, sobriety and self-improvement might prevail. This was certainly behind his decision to move to Saltaire, where he could lay down his own bye-laws on drinking, smoking, swearing and gambling. His Club and Institute took the place of the public house, which was not allowed in the new village. Victoria Hall supplied the advantages of the pub, without the evils. There, Salt made provision for innocent rational and intelligent recreation. His public park was another similar mechanism of moral reform.

Another major motivating factor behind Titus Salt's decision to set up a model industrial community at Saltaire, can be found in the local political situation at the time. Working class alienation caused by the traumatic experiences of urban and industrial life was made manifest in bitter class conflict throughout the 1840s ('Hungry Forties'). The political economy of many early capitalists hinged upon a *laissez-faire* belief in the cash nexus and the separation of interests between masters and men. By 1848, the latter saw their salvation in the principles of the Chartist movement, which was widely and zealously supported in Bradford. During the year of Salt's office as mayor of the town, working-class Chartists were marching armed on the streets of Bradford and, for several days, controlled a sizeable part of it. By the end of 1848, political order had been restored, Chartist militants were defeated, but sensible mill owners like Salt had been sufficiently disturbed to steer, henceforth, a more harmonious course between capital and labour. Saltaire was conceived within this context of class collaboration. From that time, several employers like Titus Salt were anxious to understand their workforce and to emphasise the interface of worker and employer relationships. In the new industrial order, working men and women had to be convinced there was something in it for them other than long hours, low wages, poor housing and bad health. Saltaire was Titus Salt's guarantee of a greater harmony of interests with his workers.

Having argued for Salt's altruism with his employees, we must not lose sight of his talents as a businessman whose priority was profit. By 1850, there was a clear managerial advantage for relocating his business empire out of Bradford. Mechanised combing finally became a reality in 1845. This would necessitate bringing all the major textile processes under one roof. There were few sites available in Bradford centre sufficiently large enough for the huge manufactory Salt envisaged. It made good management sense to relocate out of Bradford where land was cheaper, water plentiful, and transport readily available.

This is the village of Copley, viewed from St Stephen's church across the river Calder. Copley is a couple of miles south west of Halifax, which, like Bradford, had become a centre of worsted cloth production by 1800. A few years prior to Titus Salt's ideas for a model industrial village at Saltaire, another West Yorkshire mill owner was thinking along the same lines. In 1844 Edward Akroyd bought an old mill and land here at Copley. He modernised the mill (1847) and erected houses for his workforce, which transferred from his rural mills at Luddendenfoot. In order to develop harmonious relations between employer and worker, Akroyd personally financed a range of communal facilities and institutions including allotment gardens, public refectory, library, school, savings bank and (here, far right) a recreation ground and co-operative store.

Calder Terrace, Copley. From 1848, and before Salt, Akroyd built 136 cottages, which eventually housed around 700 people. The earliest housing was rented at £6 per year, but proved too expensive for the mill workers. Subsequent housing was built with cheaper materials, rented out at a more acceptable £4 per annum. Unfortunately, all the houses at Copley were unhealthily back-to-back and, in some cases, the living room downstairs served as a second bedroom by means of a 'fold-away bedstead'. Their quiet rural location, however, may have given these cottages a slight advantage over their urban counterparts down the road in central Halifax.

Akroydon. While Copley fitted into the late eighteenth-century tradition of a rural mill village, Akroyd's second experiment was conceived more along the lines of a large-scale residential industrial estate, set in an urban context of self-improvement, sobriety and respectability. In 1855, and contemporary with Salt's work at Saltaire, Edward Akroyd bought an estate at Haley Hill in Halifax, where he asked the architect Gilbert Scott to design and plan an integrated community of 350 homes around a central square. The houses were to be financed by local building societies, on land donated by Akroyd. Eventually, only ninety-two houses were completed around a square with a market cross.

Salisbury Place, Akroydon. From the outset, Akroydon was conceived as a homeownership scheme. Akroyd had not accumulated the vast wealth of his entrepreneurial peer in Bradford, and thus could not afford to finance the whole scheme. Moreover, Akroyd believed passionately in thrift and homeownership as the keys to working class self-improvement. Unfortunately, the two-bedroom properties in Salisbury Place retailed in 1863 at £136 each and some larger three-bedroom housing in Chester Road at £460. Both were outside the price range of most Halifax mill workers, and, therefore, Akroydon failed as a model industrial village for a local workforce, although the mill owner supported his housing scheme with all the usual accompaniments of social and self-improvement.

All Souls church, Haley Hill, Halifax. This magnificent building was designed by Gilbert Scott for Edward Akroyd. It was built in 1856-1859 on a site over-looking Akroyd's weaving and combing sheds at Haley Hill. Close by, he estab-lished church schools, a working men's college, a literary and scientific society, a clothing club and a Life Annuity Insurance scheme.

Joseph Crossley's almshouses. By 1865, the Halifax textile empire of Edward Akroyd was in decline, overshadowed by the expanding business of John Crossley and his three sons at Dean Clough Mills. They also took up the paternalism pioneered by Akroyd and Titus Salt. Joseph Crossley built these almshouses on Arden Road.

Francis Crossley's almshouses. These twenty-six Gothic almshouses were built close to Frank Crossley's stylish mansion at Belle Vue, Halifax, in 1855. Former employees lived here rent-free, and received a small weekly pension. Close by, he provided the land and some of the finance for a Congregational Chapel.

The People's Park, Halifax. In 1856, as part of Frank Crossley's crusade for social harmony between the classes, he commissioned Joseph Paxton (designer of the Crystal Palace) to plan for him a pioneering public recreation area – the People's Park. This he then gave to the Halifax corporation, on the proviso that playing games, bathing, singing, political meetings, and even taking refreshments, were all banned.

West Hill Park estate, Halifax. The third brother, John Crossley, also worked with the Halifax Permanent Building Society to erect freehold dwellings for thrifty artisans in the Belle Vue area at Milton Terrace and Cromwell Terrace on the West Hill Park estate. By 1871, there were in excess of 200 houses, but the church, school and other facilities of social improvement were never completed, owing to John Crossley's bankruptcy.

Bradford, 1882. The town, as portrayed by the *Illustrated London News* in 1882, with the rural idyll left long behind. By that time, Bradford had become a watchword for urban squalor, poor quality housing and public health hazards.

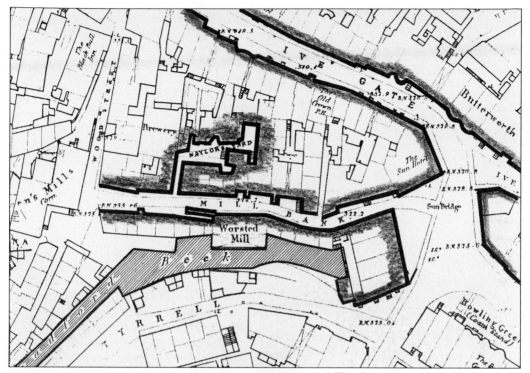

Millbank, 1846. During the first half of the nineteenth century, speculative builders dropped one-room cottages of poor quality and no services into the yards and folds of Bradford's medieval geography. This 'in-filling' of these ancient yards accommodated the town's exploding population after 1810. Naylor's yard between Ivegate and Millbank is a good example of this unhealthy trend.

Poole Alley, c.1880. This was one of hundreds of alleys, or ginnels, leading to the courts and yards of early Victorian Bradford. This one was located off Silsbridge Lane, an area noted for its high proportion of Irish immigrants. It was in narrow unhealthy corners like this that new town dwellers tried to continue their rural way of life and raise pigs, hens etc.

33

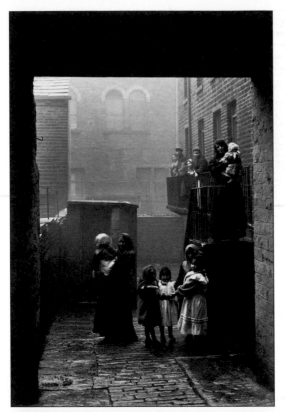

Matriarchy, near Leeds Road, 1904. Here, in a back yard near Eastbrook Hall, the matriarchy hold sway, presiding in judgement over the behaviour of their children, recycling economic information or simply having a good old gossip, a prime leisure activity of the time.

Wapping Cross Street, c.1890. Even by the end of the nineteenth century, Bradford still had its slum areas of back-to-back working class homes, many of which survived well into the next century. Here, in the Wapping area located behind the parish church, mothers keep an eye on their young children, most of whom are girls (boys were often away from home, playing in gangs or running errands for working adults).

SANITARY CONDITION OF BRADFORD.

THE WOOLCOMBERS' REPORT.

We lay before our readers the extracts we promised them last week. They are selected from those reported, and are most of them such as were read by Mr. White at the meeting on Tuesday week. In those cases where the fuel is not named, it is to be understood that it is the same as in the last case. It must also be stated, that where no figures are given, the case has nothing more than the ordinary features. The word "female" appended, intimates that there is only one female in the family.

FLINN AND HOWE'S REPORT.

Cannon Street—

Case 1. No. of family 12; No. of rooms 2; No. of beds in the house 4; No. working in the house 5; No. of females 6; sort of fuel used at work, coal; dimensions of apartments 13ft. 4in. by 14ft. 4in. Dwelling situate in an entry or passage 2ft. 10in. wide; bad drainage; family in bad health; scarcely room to pass between the beds; five persons working, and twelve, including six females, sleep in one room.

Case 2. Family 4; rooms 2; beds 2; house workers 4; female 1; size 14ft 11in by 12ft 2in; cases 3, 4, and 5, much the same circumstances, with the exception that one family use charcoal and another coke, and that the apartments are only 12ft 6in by 12ft. These cases are nearly similar. Wife of No. 5 obliged to retire to rest in the presence of the man who works in the chamber. House enclosed on both sides for private purposes, which are exposed and send forth a disagreeable odour.

Case 6. Family 11; rooms 3; beds 4; females 5; coal; size 15ft by 11ft 9in. The visitors give an appalling description of this dwelling, 6 persons work in the bedroom, 2 females sleep there; bad ventilation, no drainage, pig-stye and other nuisances.

Commercial Street—

Case 8. Family 5; rooms 2; bed 1; house worker 1; females 3; coke; size 15ft 2in by 13.

Case 12. Family 10; rooms 2; beds 3; females 4; coal; size 14ft 10in by 13ft; upper room used as a workshop for five, contains two beds for six persons, two of them females—obliged to deposit ashes in front of the door, through want of necessary accommodation.

Morperion's Row—

Case 13. Family 5; rooms 2; beds 2; house workers 4; female 1; size 12ft 3in by 11ft 2in. This is a cellar with two apartments, three feet below the surface—bad drainage, continual stench, and the ashes suffered to accumulate in front of the door. An adult male resident suddenly expired in this cellar two months back; the coroner and jury expressed their astonishment at the existence of such unhealthy place, and pledged themselves to bring it before the public, but nothing has since been done to effect that object.

Case 14. Family 8; rooms and beds 2; females 1; size as last. Four persons work and sleep in the same apartment, which also serves as kitchen, &c. A child very bad with scurvy.

5ft below the surface; three persons, including a female, sleep there.

Case 31. Family 6; a room and a bed; workers 2; female 1; charcoal.

Case 32. Family 10; rooms 2; beds 3; workers 4; females 4; coal; size 16ft by 14ft 4in. Only three beds and two sleeping apartments for ten persons; bad ventilation; great heat; in this neighbourhood no water but by purchase.

Black Abbey Fold—

Case 38. Family 6; rooms and beds 3. Four, including two females, work here; upper apartment contains two beds, two men sleep in one, and a married couple in the other.

White Abbey Fold—

Case 40. A one room cellar 4ft below the surface. In this miserable apartment, a man, his wife, and four children, sleep on one bed composed of shavings; general bad health.

Case 41. Family 8; rooms and beds 2; workers 4; females 4; coal; size 16ft by 12ft. No convenience for ashes or house refuse; inmates of an emaciated appearance.

Case 44. Family 10; rooms and beds 2; workers 5; females 4; size 16ft 6in by 11ft. In the upper room of this dwelling five persons work; in it are two beds composed of shavings, on which two males and three adult females sleep.

Case 45. Family 4; a room and bed; workers 2; females 2; size 16ft 6in by 11ft. A pool of stagnant water opposite the door; one bed, in which two young men and their mother sleep. Apartment damp.

Case 46. Same numbers as last. A wretched habitation, very dark; a pernicious smell from the coke used in working; stagnant water opposite the door.

High Street—

Case 48. A cellar six feet below the surface. This wretched cellar is a workshop for three, and a sleeping apartment for two; foul vapours from gas cinders infest the place, and a pool of stagnant water near the door.

Cells 49 and 50. 8 persons huddled together in two low damp cellar rooms with 2 beds.

Salt Pie Street, White Abbey—

Case 53. Family 5; a room and a bed; workers 2; females 3; 15ft 6in by 12ft 5in. A cellar six feet below the surface; general bad health; stagnant water before the door.

Burner's Fold, White Abbey—

Case 56. Family 8; rooms 2; bed 1; a worker; females 3; charcoal; size 15ft by 10ft 6in. This is a wretched dwelling; five persons lie on one bed on the floor of the upper apartment near the charcoal fire.

Wood Street, White Abbey—

Case 57. Family 11; rooms 2; beds 4; workers 5; females 5; coal; size 17ft by 15ft 4in. The extreme of filth and wretchedness; stagnant water near the dwelling; four persons work and sleep in a horrible hole seven feet below the surface. This case is beyond description.

Regent Street, White Abbey—

Case 62. Family 3; a room and bed; workers 2; females 2;

*Duke Street—*This street is rather better paved than the previous one, but on both sides are filthy yards, and the public necessaries shamefully filthy and neglected; a vast amount of wretchedness is to be found among the inhabitants. The remainder of the circumstances are similar to those in Queen Street.

Nelson Court—

Case 48. Family 10; a room and two beds; females 4; size 13ft by 10ft.

Case 49. Very damp, a privy within seven feet of the door. Family subject to disease, which they attribute to the filth and stench by which they are surrounded.

Union Street—

Cases 52 and 53. Twenty-five persons, including 13 females, live in four rooms 15ft 3in by 15ft. There are eleven wretched dwellings adjoining this, in which the inmates are literally crammed together in the midst of filth; no ventilation.

Case 54. Family 9; rooms and beds 2. The place is surrounded with privies.

Cross Street, George Street—

Case 91. Family 9; rooms 2; beds 3; females 4. A privy, within nine feet of the door. The walls are black with damp; pig-styes close by.

Eastbrook Terrace—

Case 92. Family 6; 1 room; 2 beds. This is a miserable cellar, in which six persons reside, and sleep near a charcoal stove. There are five cellars of the same description in the yard.

Case 96. This is a vile place; six females and two males sleep in the midst of the suffocating vapour of coke; the mother is very ill—scarcely able to speak.

Case 97. Family 8; rooms and beds 2. A wretched abode —in the upper apartment two work and eight sleep near a charcoal stove. The man has had five of his family ill at the same time, from the suffocating smell.

Lower Globe Fold—

Case 101. Family 10; rooms 2. Stagnant water in front of the door, together with ashes and night soil in large quantities—a disgusting scene. A boy ill in bed.

Case 102. Family 10; rooms 2; beds 3. Five persons work and seven sleep in the upper room. Very much crowded. They complain of bad health. Wife very ill.

Case 103. Family 10; rooms 2; beds 3. In the upper room of this dwelling are two beds near a charcoal stove; they are only eleven inches apart, and are occupied by two lodgers, a young man in the one, and an upgrown female in the other. Place extremely filthy.

Back Lane, Westgate—

Case 113. Family 5; a room and a bed; females 2. In this residence the enjoyment of health is out of the question, and little attention paid to morality or common decency.

Case 114. Family 7; 1 room; 3 beds: charcoal. A separate chamber, at which a female works at a charcoal stove. It is also a sleeping apartment for seven persons, including three females.

Sanitary report of the Woolcombers, 1845. Living conditions for many of Salt's Bradford employees had become so bad that Bradford Woolcombers actually organised and published their own report of the insanitary environment in which they lived. Titus Salt, as a major shareholder in the *Bradford Observer*, the town's leading newspaper, was all too aware of his employees' predicament.

Burial register, Horton, 1809. Killer diseases were all too frequent visitors to the ghettos of un-sewered, un-watered places like Wapping, Millbank and Goitside. Smallpox made a significant contribution to Bradford's high infant mortality after 1800.

35

Temperance pledge. For many, drunkenness was the quickest way out of Bradford, but it was also by far the most common cause of argument, misery and violence in the working-class home. Saltaire had a tradition for temperance, although Salt himself was neither teetotal nor rigorous in his personal use of alcohol. He criticised the temptations of the public house, rather than what it sold. He was a lifetime contributor to several temperance organisations and, consequently, refused to provide a pub in his model village at Saltaire.

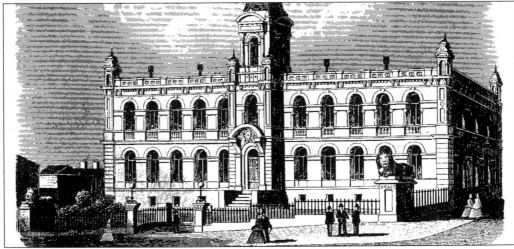

Victoria Hall, 1872. Originally this was the Saltaire Club and Institute, which Titus junior said was to 'supply the advantages of a public house, without its evils'. The building was firstly, a social club, and secondly, an educational and cultural centre. It was home to the village library, evening classes and illustrated talks and lectures. When the rules of the Club were first laid down in 1870, 'Anything tending to encourage irreligion or immorality shall be rigidly excluded; as are discussions on questions connected with controversial theology or subjects likely to excite angry feeling'.

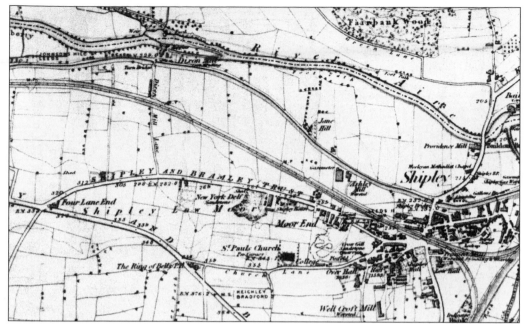

Dixon's Mill, 1846. Whatever motives lay behind Salt's decision to build a model industrial community, he had certainly made up his mind to do so by 1850, when he purchased the Dixon's Mill estate from W.R.C. Stansfield of Esholt Hall. Four miles from Bradford alongside the river Aire, the estate was made up of small walled enclosures of pastureland and an ancient corn mill. Dixon's Mill Lane ran through the site from south to north, from the Shipley-Bramley Turnpike, crossing the recently built Leeds-Skipton railway and the Leeds-Liverpool canal (1777). New York Delf quarry would provide Salt with much of his future stone-building needs.

The Mill, c.1853. It was Salt's decision to place all the processes of worsted cloth making, particularly the newly mechanised combing sector, within a single manufactory, gradually closing down his five disparate units of production in central Bradford. In 1851, the Bradford-based architects Lockwood and Mawson drew up plans for a mill costing £40,000; but they completely underestimated Salt's ambitious vision as it eventually cost nearer £100,000. William Fairburn was responsible for the engineering work in this new mill of six storeys which made up the imposing south front (550ft long), the top floor of which runs undivided the whole length of the mill. The architects were responsible for the Italianate appearance of its exterior, with twinned lantern towers of Tuscan design on either side of the Fairburn's engine-house. The ornate chimney-stack (150ft) standing apart from the mill, resembled a Tuscan campanile with its elaborate cornice (removed as unsafe in 1971).

Saltaire Mills, *c.*1884. By the time of this engraving, the New Mill (left) had been built on the north side of the first mill, which itself had been built on the site of the original corn mill. It was erected in 1868 to accommodate extra spinning capacity, so great was the demand for worsted cloth throughout the 1860s. To the right is the facade of the Congregational Sunday school, the last of Salt's public buildings (1876). Originally, the plot had been reserved for a hotel. Between the schools and the main mill building ran the railway to Leeds and Bradford as well as the allotment gardens of the workforce.

New Mill, *c.*1890. The chimney of the New Mill was modelled on the bell tower (campanile) of the Venetian church of Santa Maria Gloriosa. It has blind arches to the square tower and is topped by an octagonal arcade. Salt went to all this trouble for a smoke-emitting chimney, in order to preserve the pleasing aspect which he had created along Saltaire's main thoroughfare of Victoria Road.

Mill offices, *c*.1900. Part of the original mill, this office block overlooks the lower stretch of Victoria Road. The projecting gable (left) of this block housed Titus Salt's personal office with its private entrance. The corniced-roof line is dominated by three bell turrets (pre-buzzer days) to summon and dismiss workers at the change of shifts.

Mill opening, September 1853. This took place on Salt's fiftieth birthday, 20 September 1853, in the combing shed of the new mill which accommodated 3,500 invited guests; 2,440 of whom were his work people from Bradford. Guests of honour included the Earl of Harewood, John Shaw, mayor of Leeds, and Samuel Smith, mayor of Bradford. Salt's lavish hospitality saw 3,750 guests seated at twenty tables, where they managed to polish off: four hind quarters of beef; forty chines of beef; 120 legs of mutton; 100 dishes of lamb; forty hams; forty tongues; fifty pigeon pies; fifty dishes of roast chickens; twenty dishes of roast ducks; thirty brace of grouse; thirty brace of partridge; fifty dishes of potted meat; 320 plum puddings; 100 dishes of tartlets; 100 dishes of jelly etc, plus half a ton of potatoes, plus dessert of plums, grapes, melons, peaches, nectarines, apricots, filberts, walnuts, apples, pears, biscuits, sponge cakes etc.

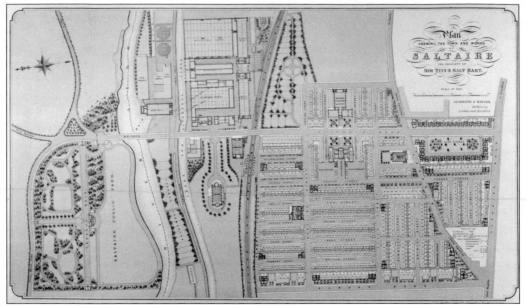

Plan of Saltaire village and mill, 1870. Between 1853 and 1870, Salt invested hundreds of thousands of pounds into the workers' housing and public buildings of his 'Utopia' on the River Aire. Lockwood and Mawson's plan of 1870 shows the completed village, with the exception of the Sunday school (1876).

Mill workers in Victoria Road, c.1865. When the mill first opened, 2,500 workers were transported into Saltaire from Bradford by special railway services hired by Salt to coincide with the shift hours at the mill. Once the house building programme was under way, workers like these would respond to the 'buzzer' in their thousands. At one time, 4,000 worked at the mill, producing 30,000 yards of cloth a day.

Three

The Original Model Village of Saltaire

Following page: Plan of Saltaire. Following the opening of the mill, work immediately began on the village and its housing. The original scheme was much more ambitious than was ever achieved. Originally, up to 10,000 people were to be accommodated and, in addition to the public buildings which were erected, a hotel, a covered market and an abattoir were intended but never completed. The architects developed their scheme around the backbone of Dixon's Mill Lane, renamed Victoria Street (later Victoria Road). The village and its public buildings eventually occupied forty-nine acres of land and were completed between 1853 and 1872. The rectangular arrangement of Saltaire was divided into separate zones for work, play, religion and home. The community actually lived on the north-facing slopes of the valley between the railway line and the Bradford-Keighley Road. Salt named the four main thoroughfares intersecting his village after Queen Victoria, Prince Albert, his wife Caroline and his son Titus (or possibly himself!). In between, streets were named (in birth order) after his children and grandchildren. His architects were each honoured with a street name (on either side of the Institute). Surprisingly, his engineer at the mill, William Fairburn, was not entitled to have a street named afer him.

The rest of the photographs in this section are identified by the lettered route around this village plan.

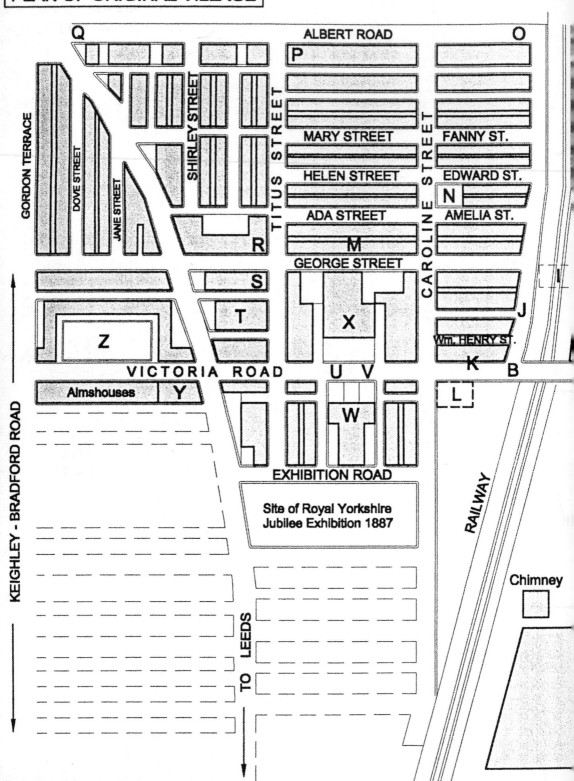

PLAN OF ORIGINAL VILLAGE

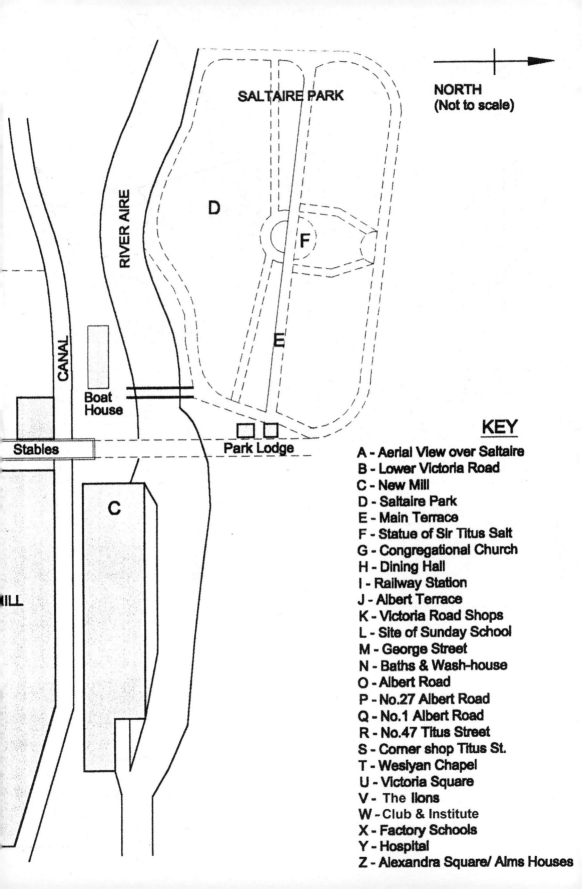

NORTH
(Not to scale)

SALTAIRE PARK

RIVER AIRE

D

F

E

CANAL

Boat House

Stables

Park Lodge

C

MILL

KEY

A - Aerial View over Saltaire
B - Lower Victoria Road
C - New Mill
D - Saltaire Park
E - Main Terrace
F - Statue of Sir Titus Salt
G - Congregational Church
H - Dining Hall
I - Railway Station
J - Albert Terrace
K - Victoria Road Shops
L - Site of Sunday School
M - George Street
N - Baths & Wash-house
O - Albert Road
P - No.27 Albert Road
Q - No.1 Albert Road
R - No.47 Titus Street
S - Corner shop Titus St.
T - Wesleyan Chapel
U - Victoria Square
V - The lions
W - Club & Institute
X - Factory Schools
Y - Hospital
Z - Alexandra Square/ Alms Houses

A. A birdseye view of Saltaire. The mill and its weaving sheds dominate the centre of this 1870 view, standing, as they do, alongside Victoria Road and opposite the Congregational church. In the top right corner of the picture, the American-style 'grid' arrangement of the houses can be discerned and, no doubt, brought some much needed discipline and order to work people more used to the chaos and insecurity of unregulated Bradford streets.

B. Victoria Road (lower). This is the main highway of Saltaire as it passes the mill and mill offices (right), moving on towards the cast iron bridge (demolished in 1962) which carried the road across the river Aire to the park, and beyond to Shipley Glen.

C. New Mill. This was built by Salt in 1868 as a spinning mill, in order to make use of excess steam power and produce even more yarn for his voracious weaving department. The mill occupied the site of the original Dixon's Mill. The original mill weir was replaced in 1871 by the current structure.

Saltaire Mill.

D. Saltaire Park, 1874. The fourteen-acre park had been opened in July 1871 and was landscaped by William Gay of Bradford. There were facilities for bowls, croquet, archery and cricket, but most visitors preferred simply to promenade between the flowerbeds and along the tree-lined walks. This very early engraving shows the main promenade and half-moon pavilion, which overlooked the cricket field.

E. Main terrace, Saltaire Park, 1875 and 1905. In the earlier picture, the shrubs, trees and flowerbeds have only recently been planted out, but by 1905 they have matured to provide a splendid public park. By 1905, the promenade was dominated by the Salt statue, the bandstand and a pair of cannons from the Battle of Trafalgar.

F. Statue of Sir Titus Salt. Erected in 1903 to commemorate the centenary of his birth, this bronze statue was commissioned by James Roberts, managing director of the mill at that time. The base shows replicas of the alpaca sheep and angora goat, the fibres of which made Sir Titus Salt a very wealthy man.

G. Congregational church. Quite deliberately sited by Salt directly opposite the mill, this church (opened in 1859) was Saltaire's first public building to be completed, at a cost to Salt of £16,000. Built in the Classical style, it is considered one of the finest buildings to originate from the Lockwood & Mawson partnership. It originally seated 600 people and regularly accommodated 400 worshippers.

H. Dining hall. Situated across Victoria Road opposite the mill, this workers' refectory can also be accessed by a tunnel from the mill yard. In the very early days, the work people were provided with subsidised food at a cheap set price: meat and potato pie – twopence; a cup of tea or coffee – one penny; a bowl of soup – a halfpenny. Workers could also cook their own food here and use the facilities for nothing. The building cost Salt £3,600 and was completed in 1854. Seating 800 diners, it proved a useful facility in the transitional move from Bradford to Saltaire, acting as a temporary school and church.

I. Railway station, c.1900. Built in 1856 as part of the recently opened Leeds-Skipton line, this station is in keeping with Lockwood and Mawson's Italianate style, which is evident throughout the whole village. This convenient little station was a victim of Lord Beeching's 'axe' in 1965 and was demolished in the early 1970's.

J. Albert Terrace, c.1984. This wonderful 'Brandtesque' photograph, from the camera of Ian Beesley, captures the rain-washed cobbles of Albert Terrace, more familiarly known as 't'railway bottom'. This was part of the first stage of house-building in Saltaire, and was completed in 1854. It took in all the streets between Caroline Street and Albert Terrace to the north and south, and between Victoria Road and Herbert Street to the east and west. To the right of this photograph are the three-storey boarding houses at the end of George Street and William Henry Street, the latter named after Salt's oldest child.

K. Shops in Victoria Road. Despite several street corner shops, this was the main shopping precinct in the original village. At the census of 1871, there were forty shops providing for a population of 4,300 people living in 824 completed houses.

L. Congregational Sunday school. This was the last of the public buildings to be erected in Saltaire, on a site opposite the main shopping area in Victoria Road. It was originally intended as a site for a hotel. The cornerstone of the school was laid on 1 May 1876 by Salt's grandsons, Gordon and Harold. It cost Salt £10,000 and could accommodate 800 scholars. It was demolished in 1972.

M. George Street. Built between 1854 and 1858, these overlookers' cottages generally consisted of scullery, kitchen, living room, cellar and two or three bedrooms. Running north to south the complete length of the village, this street afforded travellers on the Bradford Road a view of Salt's magnificent church and tower. Also special to this street are the small apron gardens in front of each house. The taller building in the middle of the row has three storeys and six bedrooms.

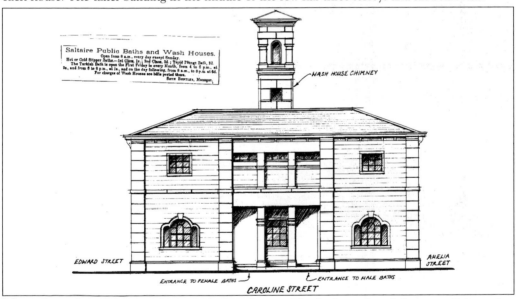

N. Baths and wash-house. Photographic evidence of the baths and wash-house at Saltaire has yet to surface. This is a conjectural illustration drawn by a professional architect from a surviving original set of plans. The original building bore little resemblance to that remembered by residents of Saltaire in the 1930s, when it served as workers' cottages. Like so much of the village, the original wash-house was strongly Italianate in style, with a colonnaded facade and a small campanile chimney. The building was located along Caroline Street, between Edward and Amelia streets, cost £7,000, and was opened in July 1863. The baths and wash-house were highly regarded by public health reformers of the day, but not popular with the inhabitants, possibly because of the small charge that was made, as well as the tenants' preference to bathe and wash clothes in their own homes. The building was closed as early as 1894, but later converted to homes and finally demolished in 1936.

O. Albert Road, *c*.1900. This is the western boundary of the village and its houses were completed in 1868 in the final phase of house building. In 1871, the houses on the right accommodated professional men and their families, not always associated with the mill. Here lived teachers, ministers and civil servants, as well as foremen at the mill. Rents here might be as high as 7s 6d per week. On the left of this photograph is the Board School, built by Shipley School Board, a little after the village, in 1874.

P. 27, Albert Road, *c*.1976. A stone cleaning programme by Bradford Corporation in 1974 distinguishes this foreman's home at the corner of Titus Street and Albert Road from the row of eighteen overlookers' cottages alongside (left). Overlooking the green fields of the Aire Valley (until 1933) and facing the setting sun, these houses offered a wonderful prospect for those who could afford the relatively modest rents which Salt charged.

Q. 1 Albert Road. The largest house in the village incurred an annual rental of £18 (7s per week). In 1871, it was occupied by the family of thirty-year-old Fred Wood, the chief cashier at Salt's mill.

R. 47 Titus Street. Having completed the housing south of Caroline Street by 1857, Salt and his architects decided to lay the streets between the Leeds Turnpike road and Titus Street, parallel to Titus Street. By running across the slope of the land rather than up and down it, the houses were visually more pleasing to the eye of the passer-by on the Leeds Road. At 47 Titus Street, almost the centre of the village, the roofline is broken by a windowed viewing tower, whose purpose is in doubt. As the house was occupied in 1871 by Sgt-Maj. Hill, the commissionaire and security officer at the mill, it is likely to have been nothing more sinister than a fire watch, although not all the village is fully visible from the top of the tower.

S. Corner shop in Titus Street. These are two typical examples of the small corner shops provided by Salt in the later development of his village. He personally vetted all those tenants who ran shops, but never interfered in their commerce.

T. Saltaire Wesleyan Methodist chapel, 1868. This was replaced by the Saltaire Methodist Church in 1973. The original building, by Lockwood & Mawson, was financed by subscriptions and collections, although Titus Salt gave the land and personally laid the foundation stone in 1866.

U. Victoria Square. This square in Victoria Road is marked at the four corners by the lion statuary of Thomas Milnes. The lions represent War, Peace, Vigilance, and Determination. They are thought to have been sculpted for the Nelson monument in Trafalgar Square.

V. The Saltaire lions. Statuary of Thomas Milnes: Vigilance and Peace.

W. Saltaire Club and Institute. This fine building makes up the east side of Victoria Square. It was completed in 1871 and cost Salt £25,000. It offered an impressive range of facilities, including a library and reading room, chess and draughts room, a smoking room, a billiard room, a lecture theatre for 800 people, a concert hall, a rifle range and drill room, and a gymnasium. Membership was cheap and it provided a home for numerous clubs and societies in the village.

X. Factory schools. These were erected in 1867 and opened in the following year. They make up the western boundary of Victoria Square, being set back from the road some twenty metres. Once again, the Italianate style prevails in the colonnaded front with its Corinthian pillars and window pilasters. Much of the ornamental stone work in the triangular pediment of the central gable was done by Thomas Milnes.

Y. Saltaire Hospital, *c*.1890. Originally, this was a small two-storey hospital of six beds built at the north east corner of Alexandra Square. It was opened in 1868 as a casualty ward for accidents at the mill, but developed into a cottage hospital for the whole community. Saltaire ran two sick benefit societies (8s a week when sick) at the modest rate of one shilling per month, of which a third was paid by the company.

Z. Alexandra Square almshouses, 1874. Adjoining the hospital, and completing this green and open little square, were forty-five almshouses built in the Venetian Gothic style. All were single-storey, with the exception of two on the east and west sides facing each other. Those on the western side house a bell turret and, under their gable ends are the monograms of TS and CS, carved in stone. Below these two houses in the north west corner, Salt provided a small private chapel for the pensioners in order to save their tired limbs on winter days. This chapel has now become another almshouse. The original buildings were opened in September 1868 and came with a weekly pension of 7s 6d for a single person and 10s for a married couple.

Four
Special Occasions and Events at Saltaire after 1876

The grand opening of the Institute, June 1872. A year earlier, the foundation stone of the Institute and Club had been laid, but in June of the following year, guests and work people were invited to a magnificent ball and musical concert. From here, Titus Salt junior later gave lantern slide shows of his travels around Europe and the Middle East, as his wife Catherine began a well supported class in 'cottage cookery'.

85. Principal guests at the mill opening in 1853. This took place on 20 September 1853 to coincide with Salt's fiftieth birthday. Here the principal guests are, from left to right: Caroline Salt, Henry Lascelles (3rd Earl of Harewood), Titus Salt, Mrs Smith (Mayoress of Bradford), and John Shaw (Mayor of Leeds).

Left: Burial of Titus Salt, 5 January 1877. Salt was interred in the family mausoleum adjoining the church. Special trains were run from the centre of Bradford until 13 January 1877 for the general public to pay their last respects. Today the mausoleum holds Salt and his wife, their children Fanny, Whitlam and Mary, as well as their youngest son, Titus, and his wife, Catherine. This is a view of the interior of the Salt mausoleum. *Right:* The joint-stock company, 1881. This advertisement of 1895 reveals that the firm had become a joint-stock company under the title of Sir Titus Salt (Bart) Sons & Co. Shares were largely restricted to family members. The first directors included Titus Salt junior, Edward Salt, and the brothers Charles and William Stead, who had been good personal friends of Sir Titus. The company was registered in July 1881 with a capital of £750,000.

Royal visit to Milner Field, 1882.
The Royal carriage awaits the
Prince and Princess of Wales in the
courtyard at Milner Field. The royal
couple, later King Edward VII and
Queen Alexandra, were guests of
Titus and Catherine Salt on the
occasion of the official opening of
the Bradford Technical College in
June of that year.

Royal tree-planting ceremony,
Saltaire Park, June 1882. The
Prince of Wales, accompanied by
Princess Alexandra, plants a tree
in Saltaire Park, in memory of its
founder. To the right are Titus
Salt junior, wife Catherine, and
their children Gordon, Lawrence
and Mary Isobel.

First Saltaire Park gala and fete, July 1885. This splendid midsummer occasion was the highlight of the social calendar for most young people in Saltaire, until well after the First World War. Funds were raised for a variety of local charities and good causes. It was organised by the Shipley and District Friendly and Trade Societies.

Royal Yorkshire Jubilee Exhibition at Saltaire, 1887. This exhibition was originally planned to raise funds for new accommodation for the Science and Arts schools at Saltaire. The governors of the Salts High School hoped to recoup the costs of a new building from the profits. The new building, at the rear of the Victoria Hall, was the centrepiece of the exhibition.

Official opening of the building and exhibition by Princess Beatrice, 6 May 1887. Titus Salt junior and members of his family welcome the Princess on the steps of the new building. Top right of the photograph is the main public entrance to the exhibition proper.

The Triumphal Arch, Victoria Road, Saltaire, 1887. Above the arch are figures representing the varieties of sheep and goats whose wools were consumed at the mill. The view looks up Victoria Road from the mill.

Princess Beatrice in 1887. The youngest child of Queen Victoria and Prince Albert, born in 1857. She had married Henry, Prince of Battenburg, in 1885 and was pregnant with her second child (a future Queen of Spain) when she came to Saltaire.

Saltaire Exhibition, c.1886. The exhibition site covered twelve acres, most of it at the rear of the present Shipley College. It was bounded by the railway to the north and by Saltaire Road to the south. There were several delays to the opening, owing to bad weather, but here, the bandstand, cafe and photographic studio are under construction. In the distance (right) can be seen the Maze and Toboggan Run, which ran parallel to the railway line.

Saltaire Exhibition gallery, 1887. The main entrance to the exhibition was south of the present college, close to the main road to Leeds and Shipley. A long covered avenue ran parallel to this road as far as Baker Street. Running at right angles to it, were a series of exhibition courts like this one, where a fine display of Doulton porcelain takes pride of place.

Exhibition stand, Hubbard collection, 1887. A display of stuffed animals and pelts from Canada and the Arctic region.

Exhibition concert hall, 1887. This was located between the new college building and the railway line. There was seating for 3,000 provided for the daily organ concerts held throughout the exhibition.

Tree-planting ceremony, May 1887. Princess Beatrice plants a small tree at Milner Field, in memory of Sir Titus Salt. Here she is attended by Titus Salt junior, his wife Catherine and their daughter Isobel. Titus Salt junior died only six months after this ceremony. He had been diagnosed with heart disease two years earlier, but his premature and unexpected death at the age of forty-four seriously damaged the Salt dynasty at the mill and at Milner Field.

Right: Salt's Mill in the hands of the receivers, September 1892. During the 1880s, there had been a growing trend in ladies' fashions, away from thick lustre cloth in alpaca and mohair, towards more light-weight soft-clinging materials, which enhanced the natural contours of the female figure. As a result, the crinoline dress passed quickly out of fashion, and with it the lustre dress goods trade on which Salt's empire had been built. This coincided with a period of world wide deflation and the onset of protectionism by the new industrial economies of France, Germany and the USA. It was the closure of the profitable American market by the McKinley tariff of 1890 that finally sent the firm at Saltaire into receivership. *Below:* New owners, Isaac Smith and John Maddocks, 1893. As the old company was wound up and Charles Stead and J. Croft were appointed as its receivers, managers and liquidators. The closure sent shock waves through the Bradford trade: it was inconceivable that the mills should be closed down completely and a whole community wiped out. The situation was resolved when four Bradford businessmen purchased the company and all its assets, promising to install new engines and machinery and to modernise the plant's commercial policy. The syndicate was chaired by Isaac Smith of Fieldhead Mills and, formerly, a mayor of Bradford. It also included John Maddocks, JP of Heaton; woolstapler John Rhodes; and James Roberts, an expert in colonial wools.

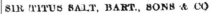

SIR TITUS SALT, BART., SONS & CO

APPLICATION FOR THE APPOINTMENT OF RECEIVERS.

Yesterday Mr. Assheton Cross, in the debenture-holders' action of Cooke v. Sir Titus Salt, Bart., Sons & Co., applied to Mr. Justice Bruce, sitting as the Vacation Judge, to appoint interim managers and receivers of this undertaking.

The company, the learned counsel said, was incorporated in July, 1881, to carry on then well-known business at Saltaire, in Yorkshire, the capital being £750,000. Three hundred thousand pounds had been issued in debenture bonds, besides which there were bonds not strictly debentures amounting altogether to £360,000, besides the debenture debt. Financial difficulties had arisen through no fault of anyone connected with the undertaking, but through changes in the United States tariff. As a rule about 4000 hands were employed, but the wages sheet had gone down to about £1200 a week. The company finding it necessary to issue a notice as to their financial condition, Mr. Cooke brought his action against the company and the trustees for the debenture-holders, on behalf of himself and other debenture-holders. Under it his Lordship had appointed *ex parte* as managers Mr. Joseph Croft, the manager of the Bradford Bank, who were creditors for £155,000, and Mr. Charles Stead, one of the directors of the company, to keep on the works and to obtain powers to borrow money, but that was not now asked. What they did ask was that his Lordship would appoint these gentlemen as joint interim receivers and managers to carry on the business as a going concern until the trial of the action. Mr. Maclaren, for the company, and Mr. Baron, for the trustees for the debenture-holders, and also, he believed, for the debenture-holders, appeared and consented to this course. To avoid trouble and expense he would ask his Lordship not to follow the usual form of order in reference to handing over the papers, books, and documents, it being understood and everybody being satisfied with an undertaking to supply copies and give them access at all times to what might be required.

His Lordship made the order thus asked for.

Left: John Maddocks. *Right:* Isaac Smith.

James Roberts survived his three other partners to become sole owner of Salts and Saltaire by 1896. Born in Haworth in 1848, the son of a local farmer, he had entered the textile industry at the age of twelve in the spinning mill of William Greenwood at Oxenhope. It was Roberts who single-handedly transformed the fortunes of the mill at Saltaire, based on a revival of the lustre trade. Roberts had been able to pay all of Salt's creditors in full and, by 1895, had returned the labour force at Saltaire to 2,500. All departments were working at full capacity by that year when a full range of goods was for sale at competitive prices and stunningly presented. In 1909, Roberts was made a baronet for his services to the textile industry.

The spinning department Salt's Mill, 1902. The decorations in the spinning mill at Saltaire mark the delayed Coronation of King Edward. Although Queen Victoria had died on 22 January 1901, her son's succession was postponed until the summer of 1902, owing to Edward's sudden illness from peritonitis.

Dining Hall, c.1900. By the turn of the twentieth century, the operatives' dining room had become redundant, as workers preferred to eat at home or bring their own 'snap'. The bricked-up windows suggest the building was permanently out of use. Above the front entrance on the huge stone medallion is Salt's coat of arms. To the left is the staircase down to the railway platform. A hoarding on the side wall of the building announces the forthcoming lecture, due to take place in the village, to be given by Prince Peter Kropotkin, a former member of the Russian aristocracy but a convert to socialism since 1872. He remained resident in England as a political refugee until the Russian revolution of 1917.

Mill overlookers on work's outing, 1905. Titus Salt had recognised early in his life that social harmony between the classes was essential for good industrial relations. As early as 1849, he had taken advantage of the new railway to transport 3,000 of his Bradford workforce for a day out at Malham and Gordale Scar in the Yorkshire Dales. James Roberts continued the tradition well into the twentieth century.

Visit of General Booth to Saltaire, July 1907. Saltaire model village caught the imagination of many Victorian social observers and politicians. Lord Palmerston visited the village as early as 1864, and John Bright came to see it in 1877. The Prime Minister of New Zealand and the ambassadors of Burma and Japan all visited at some point during Salt's lifetime. In July of 1907, Saltaire welcomed perhaps the foremost social reformer of the day, Gen. William Booth, founder of the Salvation Army. Here, aged seventy-eight, Booth salutes the large crowd from his motorcade outside the Saltaire Club and Institute in Victoria Road.

RECRUITING MEETING. SALTAIRE PARK OCT 3ᴿᴰ 1914.

Army Recruitment Meeting, Saltaire Park, October 1914. Thousands attended this public appeal for volunteers to the armed services on 3 October 1914. The response from most northern textile communities was huge. At Saltaire, by 1915, 23% of its male employees of military age were serving in the armed services including Joseph Henry Roberts, the only surviving son of managing director James Roberts. Joseph was employed at the mill as manager of the wool, dress goods and linings departments and was conscripted into the army in spite of the protestations of his influential father. He died on the Western Front, like so many of the others from the mill.

Sir James Hill, c.1918. Hill and his two sons were joined by Henry Whitehead (knighted in 1921) and Ernest Gates, a highly successful textile manufacturer with a reputation for solid business sense and keen financial acumen. It was the decision of Hill and Gates in 1923 to reconstruct the Saltaire business as a public company with the name of Salts (Saltaire) Ltd. The public company paid £3.4 million for the business and Gates became the new managing director at the age of forty-nine.

Royal visit to Saltaire, 29 May 1918. Sir James Roberts had the misfortune to outlive all his four sons and, by 1917, was finding wartime production with a diminished workforce at the mill, too great a task for one man. Consequently, in February 1918, he sold the mill and village for £2 million to a syndicate of Bradford wool men. Three months later, the new owners welcomed King George V and Queen Mary as part of a whistle-stop morale boosting tour of Yorkshire textile towns. Here, the King appears in military uniform, and is speaking to the chairman of the new company, Sir James Hill – as well as Mr Henry Whitehead and Mr Ernest Gates. Queen Mary was particularly impressed by the beautiful view of Baildon Moor and Milner Field, which the large plate glass windows of the burling department (lower mill) afforded.

Coronation tea party in Ada Street, Saltaire, 12 May 1937. Street parties like this were held up and down the land to celebrate the Coronation of King George VI and his consort, Queen Elizabeth.

Royal visit to Saltaire, 20 October 1937. Enthusiasm for the royal couple was still at a high pitch when Their Majesties decided to make a brief stay at Saltaire on their northern tour later that year. Here, managing director R.W. Guild welcomes the royal couple in a specially erected gazebo in the mill yard.

King George VI and Queen Elizabeth with directors of Salts (Saltaire) Ltd., 1937. On the extreme left of this photograph is managing director Robert Whyte Guild, formerly Scottish agent of Ernest Gates. Guild had succeeded A.R. Hollins as managing director of Salts in 1929. Guild's appointment coincided with the international economic crisis, galloping inflation, falling wool prices, and a trading loss at the mill of a quarter of a million pounds. Guild's solution was to underwrite the firm's capital valuation by £1.5 million and to sell off the housing stock of the village (1933). Having cut their losses, the partners were able to take advantage of the upturn in trade after 1931.

Royal visit, October 1937. As the royal couple take their leave of the mill, the King of England becomes just one of the crowd!

Sale of the village, 1933. This is a copy of a letter from R.W. Guild to every tenant in Saltaire in the summer of 1933: not the best of times for working people to start buying their own homes. Nevertheless, the sale went through and the capital was used to buy cap-spinning machinery. The unity of the mill village, which Sit Titus Salt had created, was broken irrevocably.

Shipley and Saltaire say 'No', 1937. The protest march, objecting to the merger of Shipley and Saltaire with Bradford Corporation, reaches its climax outside Shipley Town Hall in July 1937. The strength of public outrage was measured by the size of the turnout, ably led by the Saltaire band and fire brigade.

Burling department, Saltaire, 1953. Ladies of the burling and mending section of the mill celebrate the Coronation of Queen Elizabeth II in 1953.

R.W. Guild and Saltaire's centenary, 1953. Under Guild's leadership, the company turned loss into profit, as production increased and more up-to-date machinery was in use than ever before. The company bought up other mills across the United Kingdom. Mohair, alpaca, cashmere and botany yarns continued to be the firm's staple business, until the outbreak of war in 1939, when the mill went on to wartime production of military fabrics. The firm celebrated one hundred years of cloth manufacture in September 1953, when five special excursion trains took several thousand employees for a day trip to Blackpool. Here, Mr and Mrs Guild arrive at the centenary celebrations at the mill.

Visit of the Princess Royal to Saltaire, January 1996. HRH Princess Royal came to Saltaire to officially open the restored and refurbished exhibition building (formally the Technical College). Here, in the Saltaire Resource Base, she is joined by Patrick McDonnell (the seventh Baronet), Nicholas Salt and the college principal, Jean McAllister.

Five
Saltaire at Work

Wool sorting, c.1920. Here the bales of wool are unpacked direct from their country of origin: a large amount was imported from Australasia and South America at this time. Very experienced woolsorters separated the fleeces into various qualities: 70s, 64s, 60s and 58s etc.

Scouring, c.1950. The wool was taken from blending bins by skep and forced down a chute into scouring bowls of soap, alkali, and water, in order to remove all impurities. When dried, it was then ready for carding and combing.

Noble Combing, *c.*1950. The slivers of carded wool then passed into the Noble combing machine, which separated the long fibres (tops) from the short (noils). The top was then ready for drawing and spinning.

There were various methods of the spinning process: cap, flyer and ring spinning. This is the windowless spinning shed at Saltaire in 1947 (630 feet in length), a single room of 16,380 cap spindles and known to the operatives as the 'Lobby'.

Ring-twisting, *c.*1925. These ladies are in control of 'dolly' roller ring twisting machines, which twist single yarns together to produce stronger multifold yarns. These were transferred, by means of a winding machine, onto bobbins (pirns) that would fit into the shuttle, that carried the weft (horizontal thread between the warp (vertical thread) during the weaving process on the loom.

Weaving, *c.*1945. The Saltaire weaver worked her looms in noisy, arduous and sometimes dangerous conditions. Here, a weaver fixes a pirn of weft into a shuttle. These were boat-shaped contraptions hanging from the side of the loom.

Burling and mending, 1948. This process required young women to rectify any faults caused by the weaving process.

Dyehouse at Saltaire, c.1930. George Armstrong and his fellow workers in the unhealthy atmosphere of the dye house at Saltaire, where white pieces were brought up to the required shade.

Finishing department. This is where the cloth went through a variety of processes including drying, cropping, blowing, shrinking and pressing. The finished pieces were checked for faults and for the correct shade, rolled up, wrapped with paper and made ready for dispatch to the customer.

Pressing, c.1950. Larger pieces were wrapped around sheets of cardboard and placed in a press for twenty-four hours.

Saltaire Fire Brigade, c.1935. These volunteer employees assemble at the entrance to the mill yard. They undertook valuable fire-watching duty for the mill and the village every night throughout the Second World War. At that time, the Chief Fire Officer was George Hall and later Edward Stenson, who lived in the mill yard. Enoch Milner and George Armstrong (both of George Street) are both on parade in this photograph.

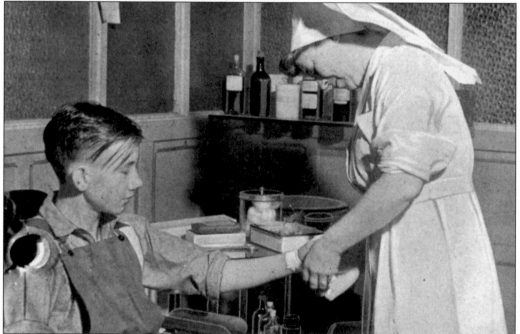

Medical provision at Saltaire Mill, c.1950. The mill clinic was equipped with a trained nursing sister , here Mrs Jones, and a male nurse in constant attendance. There were twice weekly visits by a doctor, and dental treatment was available for all insured employees. This welfare provision coincided with the post war years to provide for the growing number of displaced persons (particularly East Europeans) coming to Saltaire in search of work.

Imported female labour, 1953. After 1945, the recovery of the local worsted trade was inevitably hampered by a severe labour shortage. At Salts, the solution was to transport female workers from South Yorkshire and to accommodate them during the working week in a hostel (part of the New Mill). Also, Italian female refugees came to Saltaire Mill in large numbers, endearing themselves to the local male population by their native habit of nude bathing in the canal. Here, a young woman operates a machine winding yarn onto pirns.

Asian mill-worker, c.1960. Ultimately, the solution to the mill's labour problem after 1945 lay with the employment of large numbers of young immigrant men and women from Pakistan and India. The transition to the twenty-four-hour shift in 1951 was only facilitated by such overseas immigrant workers.

Depression and contraction in Yorkshire textiles, 1960-70. Salts (Saltaire) Ltd. was bought out by Illingworth, Morris & Company Ltd. in 1958. The mill and its operations became merely a part of a much larger textile corporation, which required the transfer of all the wool combing at Saltaire to Woolcombers Ltd. in Bradford. This signalled the end of an era of manufacturing from fleece to piece under the one roof of Saltaire mill. The new mill fell into a state of disrepair and was closed by the firm. As a signal of their faith in the site, Illingworth Morris moved their corporate headquarters to Saltaire but, for Yorkshire worsted manufacture, the writing was on the wall, as Ian Beesley's photograph graphically depicts.

Closure of the mill, 1986. After 1970, cheap foreign cloth imports, fashion change and inability to maintain investment and keep pace with new technology, all combined to depress the worsted cloth manufacture at Saltaire. In February 1986, when Illingworth Morris sold their worsted weaving interest to the Drummond mill in Bradford, production was transferred there from Saltaire. After 133 years, Titus Salt's magnificent manufactory no longer had anything to make. In 1986, Salt's massive weaving shed fell silent and deserted – an idle and empty shell fit only for the heritage trail.

Six

Saltaire at Play

Saltaire Club and Institute (Victoria Hall), 1880. This building, erected between 1869-1871, became the community's main recreational centre; Salt's substitute for the public house. The club was run by an all-male committee of sixteen, eight of whom were appointed by the mill directors and eight by the membership.

Entrance arch to Club and Institute. Essentially, this was a social club, where men over twenty-one paid an annual subscription of 10 shillings, and women and children paid 6 and 3 shillings respectively. However, Thomas Milnes' sculpted entrance arch, with classical figures representing Art and Science, tells us that classes in both were available for young men and women who had missed out on the Victorian schooling system. The building contained a school of art, a laboratory, library and reading rooms.

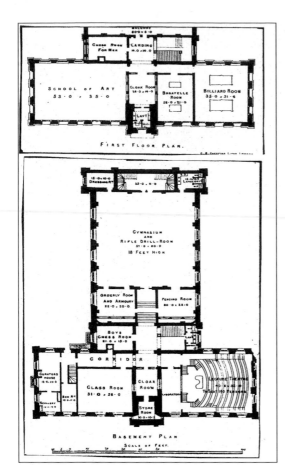

Plan of Club and Institute, 1870. For their subscription, members were entitled to an astonishingly wide range of leisure activities. These original plans of the building give a clue to this variety of provision. The lecture theatre could seat 160 and the lecture hall (i.e. the concert hall above the gymnasium) could seat 800 people. There was a fully equipped laboratory, a gymnasium and rifle drill room; billiard and bagatelle rooms; and chess and smoking rooms.

Gymnastic club, Saltaire Institute, 1915. These girls from the Salts High School are taking advantage of the fully equipped gymnasium in the basement of Victoria Hall. The gym club was later to be successful in national competitions and included members who represented their country.

Saltaire brass band, *c.*1900. The brass band movement had its origins in the Sunday school and temperance movements but, after 1850, northern mill owners like Salt and the Fosters of Black Dyke Mill also financed works bands as part of their class harmonization philosophy. Here, the Salt's mill band sport their success in the national competition.

Saltaire magazine, 1871. In the early days, the committee of the Club and Institute kept the Saltaire residents informed of a busy programme of lectures, dances and social evenings by means of a monthly magazine. This page of the magazine hints at the large number of village organizations and societies that came to make the Institute their home and headquarters. These included a choir, brass band, gymnastic club, coal club, angling club, co-operative club, horticultural society, cricket club and even the Saltaire Funeral Society (with its 2,238 living members).

SALTAIRE MEN'S SOCIETY.

FOR THE RELIEF OF THE SICK.

ESTABLISHED OCTOBER, 1866.

PRESIDENT:—Titus Salt Esq.   VICE-PRESIDENT:—Mr. John Dawson.
TREASURER:—Mr. Frederick Wood.

Members above 18 and under 25 years of age, pay 6d. per Month.
"   25   "   50   "   8d.   "

From the day of entrance, Members are entitled during Sickness, to
8s. 0d. per week for the first Six Months.
4s. 0d.   "   next   "   "
3s. 3d.   "   "   "   "
2s. 0d.   "   afterwards.

The Society has already paid to its Members during Sickness the sum of £900.
Men desirous of becoming Members to apply to FRANK HALEY, Secretary.
In addition to the payments of the Members, the Men's Society receives 4d. per month
from the Firm of Messrs. Titus Salt, Sons & Co., for every Member enrolled.

Saltaire and Shipley Angling Association.

President:—Titus Salt, Esq.
Vice-Presidents:—Messrs. Coates, Milligan and Rhind.
Honorary Secretary:—Mr. J. Child.
Secretary:—Mr. R. Illingworth.   Treasurer:—Mr. G. Morrell.
Agents:—

Mr. J. Hall, Market Street, Bradford.   Mr. Bailey, Saltaire.   Messrs. Horsman and
Hey, Shipley.

TERMS OF ADMISSION:—Gentlemen, 21s.; Tradesmen, 10s.; Working-men, 5s.
Trout Fishing begins March 1st.

SALTAIRE FIRE BRIGADE.

The following is a list of the Firemen's names and Addresses:—
Foreman, I. SHACKLETON, 29, Victoria Road.

J. M. Laughlan, 7, Fanny Street	J. Ferguson, 25, Victoria Road
J. Mitchell, 44, Mary Street	T. Light, 19, Titus Street
J. Hanson, 3, Shirley Street	S. Riley, 22, Mary Street
W. Gelder, 6, Harold Place	J. Kaye, 4, Harold Place
J. Winpenny, 26, Titus Street	T. Bairstow, 53, George Street
G. Phillipson, 42, George Street	J. Horsfall, 27, Ada Street

SALTAIRE PUBLIC DINING HALL.

Open every day, except Sunday.

Conducted on the strictest business principles, with the full intention of making it
self-supporting, so that every one may frequent it with a feeling of perfect independence.

LIST OF PRICES.

Mug of Tea or Coffee, ½d. each	Plate of Beef or Meat and Potato
Bread, 1d., 2d., and 3d.	Pie, 2d. each
Cheese or Butter, 1d. each.	Potatoes, 1d.
Bowl of Porridge or Milk, 1d. each.	Currant, Rice, or Fruit Pudding,
Bowl of Soup or Broth, 1d. each.	1d. each.

The articles supplied are all of the best quality, and as it is made a principle to
have every article fresh daily, any Broth or Soup remaining over will be sold, between
1-30 and 2 p.m. every day at half-price, to be carried away for use at home.

The Daily Local Newspapers are taken.

GEORGE MAUDSLEY, Manager.

Saltaire Public Baths and Wash Houses.

Open from 8 a.m., every day except Sunday.

Hot or Cold Slipper Baths:—1st Class, 1s.; 2nd Class, 3d.; Tepid Plunge Bath, 2d.
The Turkish Bath is open the First Friday in every Month, from 4 to 6 p.m., at
2s., and from 6 to 8 p.m., at 1s., and on the day following, from 8 a.m., to 8 p.m. at 6d.
For charges of Wash Houses see bills posted there.

SETH BENTLEY, Manager.

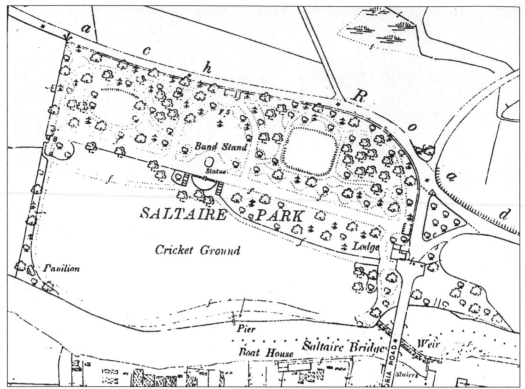

Plan of Saltaire Park. While the Institute offered a wide range of recreational activities, those villagers more athletically inclined could find satisfaction in the park at Saltaire opened in 1871. A large proportion of the fourteen acres of parkland alongside the river is taken up by the cricket field of the Saltaire Cricket Club.

Saltaire Park. The remaining acres not taken up by a cricket pitch, were laid out with shrubs, trees and plants around a number of walks and avenues with a central promenade and half-moon pavilion.

Entrance to the park. The discipline of Salt's park was strict. Beyond the wrought iron gates in the top picture can be seen a huge board of rules and regulations for behaviour in the park. Smoking was not permitted in the alcoves, and gambling and swearing were forbidden. Dogs were prohibited, as were children under eight (unless accompanied by an adult). Visitors were not to interfere with the cannons or flagpole, nor were they allowed to touch the trees and flowers. Walking on the grass borders was not permitted, nor were visitors to leave any litter lying around. Games could only be played in designated areas, and the park was evacuated at the end of each day by the ringing of the bell above the park lodge (see bottom picture).

Park Lodge, c.1920. Beyond the gateway to the left, was the private carriageway of Titus Salt junior, which led to his house at Milner Field. The public had no access to this private drive at this time. Beyond, and to the right, the Coach Road led to Ferniehurst and Baildon.

Half-Moon Pavilion, 1871. From the balcony, there was a panoramic view of the village and mill, as well as a sweeping vista across the cricket field. Below, and within the pavilion, were refreshment rooms serving afternoon teas.

Park Gates, Victoria Road, *c*.1900. In this photograph, the park entrance is to the right, beyond the closed iron gates. In the centre is the original cast iron bridge, which carried Victoria Road across the river Aire. In the distance can be seen the mill and the tower of the Institute.

Saltaire boathouse, c.1900. The boathouse was built in 1871, at around the same time as the park. This was also when the old Dixon's Mill weir was replaced and the river widened at this point, to permit leisure boating and swimming from a small pier, seen here.

Sports days in the park, 1913. The Salts High School held its sports day in the park before 1914 and below, young athletes are presented with their prizes, while above, at the village sports day, things are no less competitive.

Saltaire Cricket Club, 1916. From the very outset, the cricket field at Saltaire was always the home of the Saltaire Cricket Club, founded in 1865. At this time, it had 140 members, and was a founder club of the Bradford Cricket League. The mill provides an impressive backdrop to this game in progress in the summer of 1916.

Saltaire Cricket Pavilion, c. 1918. Members of the cricket club committee pose before the entrance of this newly built pavilion and score board, just after the First World War. Several cricketing legends have crossed its threshold including Sid Barnes, Jim Laker and R.G. Barlow, all of whom played test cricket for England.

Roberts Park, 1920. Saltaire Park became Roberts Park in October 1920, when it was presented to Bradford Corporation by Sir James Roberts as a memorial to his son, Bertram Foster Roberts.

Teachers of the Congregational Sunday school, c.1890. Like most non-conformist chapels and churches, the Saltaire Congregational church offered an infrastructure of social events and activities. Here, the women teachers of the Sunday school pose alongside the church, prior to their annual excursion, in 1890.

Congregational church choir, 1892. This photograph of the choir was taken in Saltaire Park in 1892. According to the owner of the photograph, there are two members of the Salt family somewhere in the group: one was the choirmaster and the other the church organist. Certainly, the minister is in attendance.

Works trip, c.1900. The tradition of the annual works outing, introduced by Titus Salt, was continued long after his death and well into the next century. Here, mill girls in their Sunday best enjoy a day out at Bolton Abbey.

Roberts Park and Saltaire boathouse, 1915. Families and friends enjoy the Bank Holiday atmosphere at the river jetty in Roberts Park in the high summer of 1915. It's 'all aboard' the steam tug *Rose of Saltaire* for a gentle cruise up the River Aire towards Hirst Wood, and an escape from all the cares and worries of the war.

Leisure time at Milner Field, *c*.1890. Leisure pursuits across the valley from Saltaire in the rural retreat of Milner Field were perhaps a little more respectable ...

... or were they? Young men at ease in the conservatory at Milner Field, c.1890.

Saltaire picture house. The cinema symbolised the growth of mass leisure industries after 1918. Built in 1922, outside the boundary of Saltaire village, on the Bradford-Keighley road, this cinema clearly catered for the people of Saltaire and the western suburbs of Shipley. It could seat 1,500 people, and later became the Gaumont cinema. It closed in 1957 and was demolished shortly afterwards.

Salts (Saltaire) playing fields. In 1923, the company had reorganised as Salts (Saltaire) Ltd. And, under the careful guidance of a succession of good managing directors, Gates, Hollins, Whitehead and R.H. Guild, it prospered throughout the difficult decades after the First World War. Consequently, in 1924 the company bought back from Shipley council thirty-one acres of land between the church and Hirst Wood, which it converted to playing fields for tennis, bowls, cricket and soccer. In 1937, Salts (Saltaire) Ltd completed the site with the erection of this new club house and social centre. The paternalistic example and the traditions of the famous founder of Saltaire were alive and well.

Tennis courts, Salts playing fields, *c.*1935. The club house was built on the site between the two pavilions in this picture, overlooking the tennis courts provided by the firm in 1925.

Salts (Saltaire) Cricket Club, *c*.1955. This picturesque ground was popular with visitors and, on match days in the 1950s, there were plenty of those, as both Salts and the Saltaire club were members of the Bradford Cricket League.

Salts FC, 1953. This club had its golden years in the 1950s, but its origins lie in a works team at Saltaire Mill which played at Hirst Wood before 1914. The mill's purchase of the playing fields in 1924 brought into being this club, which made great progress in the Bradford Amateur League under the captaincy and leadership of Fred Armstrong. By 1948, the club had won the West Riding Challenge Cup, the Bradford & District Cup and had even played in the FA Amateur Cup. During the years 1950-1959, this team swept almost all before it.

Saltaire Congregational ladies' keep fit class, 1938. This was run by Miss Alice Pickles (front row, centre) and includes her sister, Miss Carrie Pickles (back row, third from left), who was an international gymnast. The minister's wife, Mrs McLellan, is seated in the centre of the group.

Salts (Saltaire) brass band, 1937. In 1937, the band was once again victorious in the national championships. The cloth for their brown and yellow uniforms was manufactured in the mill, before which they pose for the local press.

Seven

Saltaire Between the Wars: 1914-1945

The First World War initially made deep inroads into the export business of the Saltaire mills, but the manufacture of uniforms and blankets for the armed services soon put the mill back on full production, as did Sir James Roberts' shrewd trade links with pre-communist Russia. However, the swift return to posterity in the immediate post-war years proved illusory, as national exports of wool and worsted dropped from £139.5 million in 1920 to only £62 million in 1921. By that time, the mill at Saltaire was in the astute business hands of Ernest Gates. Under his guidance, the end of the war at Saltaire signalled a new phase of expansion and reinvestment. The mill was extended and the labour force was reinforced by the large-scale importation of workers (mainly female) from South Yorkshire. The 1921 coal strike caused a temporary closure of the mill, when 2,000 operatives were laid off. Gates increasingly came round to a protectionist policy, and succeeded in getting the Bradford Chamber of Commerce to revoke its free trade principles during his year as president in 1923. For many small Bradford textile businesses, this came too late, as 400 firms had closed down in the 1920s and 60,000 of its workers were on the dole. During this period, Salt's (Saltaire) Ltd. (it had gone public in July 1923) traded mainly in mohair, alpaca, cashmere and worsted yarns for spinning and in plain, fancy worsted and mohair finished cloths. In 1931, these were the very fibres to benefit from the government's depreciation of sterling and the introduction of fifty per cent import duties on foreign goods.

The early death of Ernest Gates was a cruel blow to the financial security of the business in the turbulent inter-war years. His successors as managing director – R. Hollins, and, in 1929, Sir Henry Whitehead – struggled with short-time working, continental dumping and a lack of coal, during the General Strike of 1926. In 1929, Robert Whyte Guild was made managing director of the company, and he it was who steered the business into calmer, more profitable waters. In 1929, the mill was almost at a standstill and was trading at a loss of £287,000. Aided by government policies, Guild was able to direct the firm into a long period of prosperity. As order books filled, more machinery came into use, and a nightshift was introduced in 1933. Smaller businesses were bought and merged into the parent company to facilitate the diversification policy. John Wright Ltd. of Keighley (1930) and the Pepper, Lee & Co. (1936) of Dudley Hill in Bradford, were added in 1937 to the spinning potential of the Irish Worsted Mills of Portaloise in County Offaly. On the eve of the Second World War, Salt's (Saltaire) Ltd were in relatively good economic shape and on a sound financial footing, thanks to the industry of its workforce and to the leadership of R.W. Guild, its managing director.

'Mill's out', c.1920. As the buzzer blows and a shift finishes, hundreds pour out from the mill yard. The end of the First World War, on 11 November 1918, was signalled by a loud blast on the new buzzer at the mill. The noise was sufficiently loud to silence a band concert three miles away in Lister Park, Bradford. At this time, 2,700 workers at the mill operated 700 looms and 100,000 spindles. Amongst the younger women here, the shawl seems to be making way for the tam o'shanter as fashionable headwear.

R.A.M.C. Convention at Saltaire Institute, 1915. Young cadets (some merely boys) of the Army Medical Corps assemble at the Saltaire Institute for preliminary training in the spring of 1915. None would envisage the horrors of the Somme that many of them were to soon experience.

Gordon Terrace, c.1914. Municipal public transport schemes of trams and trolleybuses linked Saltaire with the growing conurbations of Shipley and Bradford after 1900, well served by the busy Keighley-Bradford road. Gordon Terrace became a thriving shopping parade for locals and visitors alike.

Gordon Terrace, c.1900. A cart delivers flour to private residences in Gordon Terrace at the turn of the century.

Gordon Terrace, c. 1910. The houses were converted to shops, in order to create a second retailing sector in the model village.

Charlesworth's shop, Gordon Terrace, 1914. John Charlesworth's grocery store, at the junction of Saltaire Road and Gordon Terrace, was popular with Saltaire's Edwardian shoppers. Charlesworth had first begun retailing as a flour dealer at No. 1 Victoria Road c.1880. Next door was Metcalfe's chemist shop.

Rosse hotel, c.1905. This public house at the roundabout junction of Saltaire Road and Keighley Road, continued to tempt Saltaire's teetotal residents. This scene, before the First World War, evokes an era of horse-drawn transport, an era that was soon to pass.

First electric tram to Saltaire, 1902.
Bradford Corporation first experimented
with horse-drawn trams and steam
trams, before introducing electric trams
in 1898. By April 1902, the service at
last reached Saltaire. Here, at Gordon
Terrace, Alderman James Hill takes the
steering handle.

Tram shed, Saltaire, c.1920. Its six bays were built in 1904 to house thirty tram cars and, after
1939, to store Bradford Corporation trolleybuses.

New mill and bridge, c.1930. Each Bank Holiday, the old cast iron bridge carried thousands of visitors to their favourite beauty spots of Shipley Glen and Baildon Moor. By 1943 it was closed to traffic, and, by 1955, it was even unsafe for pedestrians. It was replaced in 1958 by a foot-bridge.

Village sports, Roberts Park, c.1920. The park continued to be a major centre of community life in Saltaire between the wars. During the 1920s, the company purchased thirty-one acres of land beyond the church, between the canal and the river, and there developed facilities for tennis, cricket, bowling and football.

Congregational church, *c*.1940. The grandeur and magnificence of this elegant Victorian building was still evident throughout the twentieth century.

Interior of the Congregational church, *c*.1950. The barrel ceiling is divided into compartments of ornate plasterwork. The walls are held by pilasters of green marbled scagliola. The oak pews are original and the two gilt chandeliers are by Hausburg of Liverpool. The original organ was made by Holts of Leeds. This view is taken from Salt's private balcony at the back of the church, although he was rarely present; preferring to worship nearer Crow Nest at the Lightcliffe Congregational church.

Saltaire Infirmary, c.1930. The original two-storey six-bed building of 1868 was enlarged to seventeen beds and three floors in 1909. It served as an auxiliary military hospital in 1914-1918, and in 1926-1927, further extensions gave a total of twenty-four beds. The darker shade of the stonework identifies the original building in this photograph.

Factory schools become high schools, 1876. Originally, these schools provided elementary education for 700 boys and girls, many of them half-timers from the Saltaire mill. After 1870, responsibility for elementary education passed to the newly created school boards, such as the one at Shipley. These schools, financed by a new trust set up by Lady Salt and her son, Titus, became the Salt's High Schools for Boys and Girls, supplying education at a secondary level for children in the Shipley area. Titus Salt junior was the first chairman of the Shipley school board, and gave land in Albert Road for a new elementary board school there.

Boys of Salts High School, 1925. The school offered a few privileged boys and girls the chance to climb an educational ladder to university. Here, a handful of boys are sitting the school certificate examination to begin that climb.

Winders at Saltaire in 1930. For the majority of children, staying on at school was not an option. Here, fourteen-year-old Lilian Marsden and her friend, Phyllis, pose proudly for the camera. The string around Lilian's waist holds a metal hook, which was used to wind the yarn on to the spinning frame.

Mill girls outside the wash-house, 1926. Until 1921, the 'half-time' system permitted some of these young women to work half a day at school at the age of twelve. For all his enlightenment, child labour was commonplace at Saltaire mill during Titus Salt's lifetime. The girls look old before their time despite their camera 'smiles'. Many of these girls lived in the converted wash-house homes of Amelia Street and Edward Street.

Willie Cox's firewood cart, c.1900. Before the development of modern consumerism and shop retailing, markets and street hawkers like Cox were the mainstay of most working class 'shopping'. Cox lived at Baildon, but made a living selling firewood and kindling around the streets of Saltaire. Other Saltaire street characters of the inter-war years included Maurice Milton (milkman), Billy Goodison (greengrocer), Jack Nichols (coalman), Mrs Hyden (?) of Ada Street (knocker-up) and Mr Tweedy (lamp-lighter). Schofield's delivered papers and Mr Marsh cleaned windows. Henry Jukes worked full time in the mill's combing department, but in his spare time sold pie and peas (winter) and ice-cream (summer) from a small wooden push cart. His ice-cream was made in the back yard of his home at 5 Caroline Street.

Saltaire station, c.1948. An unnamed Midland Railway Stanier Class steams past Saltaire Mill and into the station. The station was closed in 1956 but reopened in 1984.

Mary Ann Cox and William, c.1918. While Saltaire was a transient experiment in industrial living and in Victorian class relationships, as well as a means to wealth and prosperity for its founder, it was always, and still is, all about people and individuals who lived, loved and worked there. These were people such as Mary Ann Cox of 9 Caroline Street, whose husband was in military service when this photograph was taken, probably around 1918.

The Bailey family of Albert Road. Single-handedly, Mrs Bailey raised seven boys and four girls at 25 Albert Road. All eleven of her children worked in the mill at Saltaire at one time or another, during the last quarter of the nineteenth century. Here, they all pose in the photographic studio of Mr Dobson of 8 Saltaire Road, in 1897.

George and Sarah Armstrong of George Street. George Armstrong lodged in a house in Amelia Street, and worked in the dyehouse at Saltaire mill in 1910, when he met his wife Sarah Godfrey, who also worked at the mill and lodged in Daisy Place. A year later they married, and moved into a company house in William Henry Street. Having joined the Saltaire Fire Brigade, Armstrong was entitled to a house with a garden at 58 George Street. In 1915, he left behind his young wife and two sons (the youngest, still a babe in arms) to fight on the Western Front. On a brief, but precious leave he posed for this photograph with his young family.

Armstrong family reunion at 58 George Street, Easter 1930. Back home, Armstrong faced a period of economic breakdown and social dislocation. In a swiftly changing world, there were few incentives for an 'old soldier' like him. People like the Armstrongs resigned themselves to surviving, getting by and coping with life as best they could among their family and friends. Here, outside their George Street home, they rest on Easter Monday 1930, following a visit to the funfair at the Tide Field in nearby Shipley. Shell-shocked Uncle Willie sits on the wall (left), behind him, George (with baby) is surrounded by his loved ones, sisters, wife, children and cousins.

Wedding of Clara Armstrong at Saltaire Congregational church, 1946. After the war, Sarah Armstrong gave birth to two daughters, Clara and Dorothy. At the end of the Second World War, Clara married able seaman Raymond Browne at the local Congregational church. Albert Terrace is visible in the background. George and Sarah (back row) look on, proud of the achievements of their two daughters.

Golden wedding anniversary, 1961. Here, children and grandchildren (none of whom lived or worked in Saltaire) surround George and Sarah on the occasion of their golden wedding anniversary, outside the familiar front door of their home of forty-eight years, a home which now belonged to them outright. Sadly, they both died within a short time of each other two years later. Their deaths epitomised the passing of a Saltaire community culture, a way of industrial living fostered by Saltaire, its inhabitants and its founder, a way of life that was about to fragment and disappear for ever.

Eight
Saltaire and Milner Field

Saltaire from the north west, c.1870. As Titus Salt's mill and model village neared completion by 1870, it was fitting that the family of Saltaire's paternalistic benefactor should live nearby. Sir Titus was already well established at Crow Nest near Lightcliffe, but in 1870, he purchased for his youngest son, Titus, the small Gilstead estate of Milner Field, a mile north-west of Saltaire, and in a commanding position overlooking the river Aire.

Old Milner Field, *c*.1800. Since the early seventeenth century, the site had been dominated by a typical West Yorkshire yeoman property, home to the ancient Bingley families of the Milners and the Oldfields. It was occupied for many decades by the Fell family, and later passed to Arthur Duncombe, who reportedly sold it and its forty-five acres to Titus Salt for £21,000.

Milner Field, 1873. Titus Salt junior demolished the old homestead and replaced it with what one writer has described as a 'Wagnerian Gothic Retreat'. Here, a circuitous drive through thick woodland, ends at the forbidding entrance arch to the rear courtyard.

Carriage drive between Saltaire and Milner Field, c.1900. This began at the park lodge, where a private road led westwards below Shipley Glen, past Trench Farm and Fell Wood to the South Lodge, one of four lodges securing the property perimeter.

South Lodge, 1922. Better known locally as the 'bottom lodge', and traditionally tenanted by the under gardener and his family. The property originally contained a porch, sitting room, kitchen, larder and two bedrooms. Edna Mills recalls life there in the early 1920s when 'it was very isolated, my mother often seeing only the milkman as he went to Saltaire from Milner Field farm, in a whole week. I remember Sir Ernest Gates had a son, I used to open the gates for their cars when they came home from Saltaire'.

A view from the park at Milner Field, *c.*1920. This view of Gothic towers peeping through the woodland, was the distant view available to most villagers of Saltaire. Once into the grounds of Milner Field, the mill and village could not be seen. The harsh world of industry and manufactory was deliberately shut out from this rural retreat.

Rear courtyard and entrance to Milner Field, 1922. Passing through the outer porch and vestibule in the centre of this picture, you arrived in the entrance hall. The rooms on the ground floor to the left were entirely functional, and given over to the preparation of food or the heating of the house.

118

Entrance hall, c.1920. The entrance hall was dominated by the three-manual organ, built to Titus Salt's request by the Sheffield organ builders, Brindley and Foster. The arches in the centre of this photograph led off to the family's private apartments, the drawing room, billiard room and the main staircase to the first floor.

Library, c.1880. Elaborate plasterwork prevails throughout this well lit period room, which overlooks the main terrace. The room is dominated by a heavily carved marble fireplace and the furniture and fittings throughout are 'baroque'.

Billiard room, c.1920. Pre-Raphaelite stained glass and murals provide the backdrop to this magnificent games room, no doubt utilised by Edward, Prince of Wales, when he was a house guest in the summer of 1882.

Staircase hall, c.1880. The suit of armour on the extreme left is armed with what suspiciously resembles a billiard cue (the billiard room is, after all, next door). This over-ornamented hallway is further reinforced by the elaborately carved wooden staircase leading to nine first floor bedrooms.

Drawing room, c.1880. Within the house at Milner Field, no expense was spared on fixtures and fittings. Oak, mahogany and cedarwood panelling, as well as thick Turkey carpeting, was to be found in most rooms. Here, the main living room is typically cluttered, the Victorians being considered the first mass consumer society.

Dining room, c.1880. The house was well served with many modern conveniences including its own water supply drawn from natural springs. It had its own filter beds for sewage disposal and an elaborate electric lighting system. Here in the dining room, adjoining the functional buildings of kitchen, pantry, dairy and servery, there are obvious clues to the influence of the Art and Crafts movement.

South Terrace, c.1920. This view shows garden walks and conservatory. The corner of the house adjoining the conservatory housed the private study and bedroom, used by the Prince of Wales on his visit in 1882.

North side of the house. This shows winter gardens and conservatory in 1922. Edna Mills' father had responsibility for the winter gardens i.e. twelve greenhouses, which were: 'big glass houses with eucalyptus trees and many flowers and shrubs. I thought it a magical place'.

The approach to the conservatory. Titus Salt junior followed his father's lead in so many aspects of life and business, that it was perhaps inevitable he would share his father's interest and hobby in the cultivation of exotic fruits. At Crow Nest, Salt senior had built several glasshouses for his personal favourite, the banana. Edward Salt was personally responsible for raising an extensive collection of orchids under glass at Ferniehurst in Baildon, while Titus Salt junior cultivated oranges in this approach way to the massive barrel-roofed conservatory at Milner Field.

Winter Garden. Elsewhere twelve greenhouses in the winter garden were home to Titus Salt's collection of rare orchids.

The conservatory, Milner Field. After 1860, improvements in obtaining artificial heat and a reduction in the price of glass facilitated the trend among the industrial 'nouveaux riches' for glass houses and conservatories. Titus Salt junior was both architect and builder of the enormous conservatory (500 square yards) adjoining the mansion at Milner Field, which came to house ornamental foliaged plants from all parts of the world including tree ferns, palms, yuccas, phormia and border planting of camellias, lapageria rosea etc. The conservatory had a mosaic floor and several life-sized marble statues.

The grounds at Milner Field. In 1870, these had been laid out and designed by Robert Marnock, who fronted the house with a terrace and promenade, which accessed a fairly orthodox parkland to the south of the house, interspersed with clumps of plants and shrubs. On the northern side, the long approach to the house first passed through deep woodland, then a small lake and boathouse (here), finally approaching the courtyard by crossing a man-made rampart.

Gateway to gardens and park. This is the gateway to the original Milner Field house of the seventeenth century.

Riding out from Milner Field, *c*.1880. About to leave the courtyard, via the ivy clad arch, is a young member of the Salt family, possibly Isobel Salt, grandaughter to Sir Titus.

Catherine Salt. Following the premature death of her husband, Titus, in November 1887, Catherine Salt and her four children, Gordon, Harold, Lawrence and Isobel, continued to play an active part in the daily life of Saltaire, until their departure from Milner Field in 1904. As a governor of the Bradford Girls' Grammar School, and a trustee of several local charities, Catherine was able to keep in touch with the community until her death in 1930, when she was buried alongside her husband in the family mausoleum at Saltaire.

Milner Field, south front.

View of Saltaire 1900. This is the view of Saltaire mill and village from the parkland at Milner Field *c.*1900.